MABLEY MCDONNELL

THE ULTIMATE TREADMILL GUIDE FOR WORKOUT

First published by MABLEY MCDONNELL 2022

Copyright © 2022 by MABLEY MCDONNELL

All rights reserved. No part of this publication may be reproduced, stored or transmitted in any form or by any means, electronic, mechanical, photocopying, recording, scanning, or otherwise without written permission from the publisher. It is illegal to copy this book, post it to a website, or distribute it by any other means without permission.

This novel is entirely a work of fiction. The names, characters and incidents portrayed in it are the work of the author's imagination. Any resemblance to actual persons, living or dead, events or localities is entirely coincidental.

MABLEY MCDONNELL asserts the moral right to be identified as the author of this work.

MABLEY MCDONNELL has no responsibility for the persistence or accuracy of URLs for external or third-party Internet Websites referred to in this publication and does not guarantee that any content on such Websites is, or will remain, accurate or appropriate.

Designations used by companies to distinguish their products are often claimed as trademarks. All brand names and product names used in this book and on its cover are trade names, service marks, trademarks and registered trademarks of their respective owners. The publishers and the book are not associated with any product or vendor mentioned in this book. None of the companies referenced within the book have endorsed the book.

First edition

*This book was professionally typeset on Reedsy
Find out more at reedsy.com*

Contents

CHAPTER 1 ....WHAT Pulse Screens WORK WITH FIT 1

CHAPTER 2...........RANCHERS Stroll ON A TREADMILL 7

CHAPTER 3.................BEST TREADMILL FOR Youngsters 18

CHAPTER 4...........TREADMILL Exercises FOR Greater BUTT Best Exercise 32

CHAPTER 5.........TREADMILL Exercise For Soccer Players....39

CHAPTER 6...........COMMON TREADMILL Wounds CAUSES AND Extreme Manual for Keep away from THEM 48

CHAPTER 7.........ADVANTAGES Of Submerged Treadmill 57

CHAPTER 8............TREADMILL In Loft Most Significant Interesting Points 67

CHAPTER 9......................THE Most effective Method To Even out A Treadmill 78

CHAPTER 10..................THE Most Effective Method to Prepare For The Signal Test On A Treadmill Scarcely any Straightforward Advances 84

CHAPTER 11................. CAN I Plug My TREADMILL Into A Standard Outlet 92

CHAPTER 12..................STEP By Step Instructions To KEEP YOURSELF AND YOUR Children SAFE AROUND A HOME TREADMILL 99

CHAPTER 13................ STEP by step Instructions To Gather Maxkare Treadmill 111

CHAPTER 14...............INSTRUCTIONS To Pick Either Collapsing AND NON-Collapsing TREADMILL......................... 119

CHAPTER 15...............INSTRUCTIONS to Let Know If TREADMILL Engine IS Terrible 127

CHAPTER 16...............INSTRUCTIONS To Supplant Treadmill Belt.. 140

1.
2.
3.
4.
5.
6.
7.
8.
9.
10.
11.
12.
13.
14.
15.

CHAPTER 1..................WHAT Pulse Screens WORK WITH FIT

These days, you can utilize numerous wellness GPS beacons to screen and track your pulse while preparing, on account of the wide choice of applications and apparatuses out there. Be that as it may, iFit is the most famous choice for pulse observing, particularly with the arrival of the ActivePulse highlight. What's more, ActivePulse permits your pulse to change your treadmill slant and speed while practicing consequently. This will assist you with preparing in your particular pulse zone, guaranteeing you obtain the best outcomes from your exercise. Simultaneously, the element will assist you with performing heart preparing with your iFit-empowered machine. Notwithstanding, for that to occur, you'll require a pulse screen that is viable with the iFit program. However, just sit back and relax! In this aide, I'll assist with figuring out what pulse screens work with iFit and how to associate them to your treadmill. How about we begin.

What is iFit ActivePulse: ActivePulse is an extreme pulse practice include that permits you to arrive at the maximum capacity of your exercises relying upon a continuous criticism circle between your treadmill's speed and slope and your deliberate pulse. Subsequently, you don't need to rely upon your machine just to get a precise estimation of your treadmill preparing power. For instance, assuming that you're playing out an iFit exercise on your treadmill, ActivePulse will help decide whether you are propelling yourself during the activity. In particular, it will let you know whether you really want to diminish or build the power. Likewise, it will naturally change your exercise hardware to that obstruction and level, hence dispensing with the requirement for self-observing.

Benefits of Dynamic Heartbeat Pulse Preparing. On the off chance that it's ActivePulse accompanies many advantages both for amateurs in the wellness business and experienced wellness lovers. To start with, ActivePulse permits you to remain in your ideal zone via naturally changing your treadmill's grade and speed. At first, the advantages of pulse preparing relied heavily on how well you would physically screen and change their work to begin in a particular zone. ActivePulse will permit you to make a constant input circle between your deliberate pulse and the machine's grade or speed. One more advantage of ActivePulse is that it adds an additional layer of customization by changing the power of your iFit preparing. This guarantees that your exercise meets your wellness necessities by utilizing progressed calculations to concentrate on your preparation designs over the long haul gradually. All the more prominently, this guarantees that your iFit exercises are set likewise from here on out. Ultimately, ActivePulse is viable with all Ifit-empowered exercise machines like NordicTrack, FreeMotion, and Proform treadmills through a programmed iFit programming update. Likewise, it will open up for other exercise machines from these brands, including rowers, bicycles, and circular coaches. In any case, on ActivePulse similarity, this element works with numerous BlueTooth pulse screens that are furnished with broadcast usefulness, which takes us to the principal question of this article. **What Pulse Screens Work with iFit:** iFit Dynamic Heartbeat viable gadgets support a few sorts of pulse screens from famous brands. In any case, before you purchase a pulse screen, it's critical to guarantee that it's viable with your wellness gear. All the more critically, you ought to check whether your wellness gear accompanies the BLE (Bluetooth Low Energy) availability include. All things considered, iFit works with Bluetooth wellness GPS beacons like the iFit SmartBeat lower arm HRM. Surprisingly better, it upholds outsider wellness and pulse screen gadgets from famous brands like Wahoo, Polar, Garmin, and some Beat gadgets.

iFit SmartBeam Lower arm Pulse screen: iFit SmartBeam is a Bluetooth-viable pulse screen that permits you to prepare all the more really. It's furnished with optical PPG innovation that detects your pulse, making it one of the most solid HRM out there. Also, you can involve it for open air exercises and runs or even sync it to the iFit pulse screen application. On the other hand, you can interface it to your iFit-empowered wellness machine and use it with the iFit licensed Dynamic Heartbeat highlight. Finally, this HRM has a customizable, non-slip band, permitting you to wear it on your upper arm or lower arm.

Featured highlights: One-size-fits-all, non-slip band Driven power button A Battery-powered Li-Particle battery endures as long as 30 hours for each charge Attractive charging link Sync to iFit-empowered gear and exercise application Bluetooth availability.

Polar iFit remote pulse screen: This gadget from Polar is one of the most adaptable wellness GPS beacons that work with iFit. It works with various smartwatches and well known wellness applications like Nike and Strava. Also, you can utilize it while performing exercise practices like swimming, paddling, treadmill running, and so forth. One more fascinating component about this pulse GPS beacon is its high precision. Likewise, it has different association choices, including ANT+ and Bluetooth network. By and large, this Polar wellness pulse screen is a great gadget for following your exercises with the iFit work out regime. The best part is that its chest tie configuration has a simple to-utilize clasp and silicone spots that watch out for it while you're preparing. **Featured highlights:** Works with generally brilliant and sports watches Viable with iOS and Android cell phones Bluetooth 4.0 ability Steady and exact pulse following Helpful chest lash plan.

Wahoo iFit Pulse screen: The Wahoo chest tie wellness, and pulse screen is one of the lightest pulse GPS beacons that work with iFit. Moreover, its wellness application can quantify ongoing exercise measurements like calorie consume and pulse. This gadget can in any case send those measurements to viable third wellness applications. Discussing similarity, this gadget can be associated remotely both to GPS gadgets and cell phones, on account of its double band ANT+ and Bluetooth usefulness. This permits you to interface up to 3 Bluetooth associations at the same time for a helpful exercise. Furthermore, the gadget has a tie association and a front sensor. Simultaneously, this incorporated chest tie configuration gives a safer fit to keep the screen from moving or sliding while at the same time working out. **Featured Highlights:**

Continuous pulse and calorie consume following Coordinated sensor and chest lash plan ANT+ and Bluetooth capacity Thin and lightweight plan Works with well known wellness applications, including the iFit application.

The most effective method to Associate iFit Pulse Screen. Any pulse screen I've recorded above works with iFit-empowered exercise gear. Be that as it may, in the event that you're encountering some trouble attempting to interface your new pulse screen to iFit, follow these means. To start with, open your pulse screen manual aide and painstakingly read how to utilize it. Then, put the gadget around your chest or lower arm, as per the manual aide. Turn on your pulse screen and stand by a couple of moments until your iFit-empowered wellness hardware naturally examines and interfaces with the gadget's Bluetooth. Pick your ideal iFit exercise as per your body necessities and select the play button. Begin your warm meeting and tap the 'End warm-up' choice when you are finished. Presently, you can begin partaking in your exercise and the advantages of pulse preparing. When the gadget is associated, you'll begin seeing your pulse readings inside your activity measurements.

End: To summarize, finding a pulse screen that works with i Fit is an extraordinary method for partaking in the advantages of the Active Pulse highlight. The best part is that it will assist you with rethinking your wellness objectives since it permits you to practice at the ideal pulse zones. Likewise, pulse preparing is one of the most mind-blowing ways of accomplishing reliable and quantifiable advancement as you mean to work on your general well being.

Habitually Sought clarification on some pressing questions.
Question-1. What are wellness trackers viable with i Fit?
i Fit is presently viable with various wellness following projects accessible to keep your exercise in one spot. For instance, it works with famous work out regimes like Strata, Apple Well being, Google Fit, and Margin Associate.

Question-2. Does i Fit follow pulse?
For i Fit to show pulse, you'll require an i Fit-viable gadget that works with your exercise machine for exact and reliable pulse perusing. You can utilize Bluetooth-empowered wellness gear, i Fit wearable, or a brilliant gadget.

Question-3. Which pulse screen works with Nordic Track?
i Fit's Smart Beat Lower arm HEM is the best pulse screen that works with Nordic Track wellness hardware.

Question-4. Does Margin's pulse screen work with i Fit?
Indeed, i Fit works with Margin remote pulse screens and even interfaces with Margin Associate. Also, the accounts in Margin Associate will adjust to i Fit, keeping your refreshed exercise history in the i Fit application.

CHAPTER 2………..RANCHERS Stroll ON A TREADMILL

Customarily, developments like the ranchers walk were just finished by bad-to-the-bone strength competitors. However, lately, such activities have turned into a standard among wellness fans hoping to work on their wellbeing. As a matter of fact, the rancher' walk is viewed as the least demanding yet the most special activity anybody can do. Because of its capacity to guarantee full-body improvement since it draws in muscles all through the whole body. To summarize, this utilitarian exercise will assist with working on your body's exhibition in an extremely straightforward way. However, might you at any point do a rancher's stroll on a treadmill? Indeed, that is the very thing that I'll be attempting to address in this aide. To begin with, this is the very thing that you want to be aware of the rancher's stroll before you integrate it into your treadmill gym routine everyday practice.

What's a Rancher's Walk: The rancher's walk/rancher's convey alludes to a strength and molding exercise that includes holding a heavyweight in each hand as you stroll for a particular distance. For example, you can convey significant burdens like free weights or iron weights in two hands and stroll forward in an orderly fashion for a specific term/distance. Then again, you can utilize different devices like committed rancher's walk handles, free weights, or a snare bar. Subsequent to strolling the given distance or running out of strolling space, put the loads down and rehash the stroll in the inverse. So, this exercise is extremely simple however very powerful. In particular, a rancher's walk is a full-body exercise that gives a superb cardio improvement while connecting a large portion of the significant muscles. Along these lines, this exercise will make you more grounded, increment your oxygen consumption, support your pulse and assist you with consuming lots of calories. Even better, it's kind with the joints, has not many specialized requests, and should be possible. As such, a rancher's walk is one of the most practical activities to do, no matter what your wellness objectives.

Rancher's Walk Advantages.
As referenced before, the rancher's walk is a full-body exercise with a few expected benefits. These advantages were first found by a previous All-American disk hurler known as John Dan. Tragically, many individuals are as yet reluctant to attempt this incredible activity, passing up its advantages. For example, a solitary rancher's walk exercise can assist you with shedding a few additional pounds, fabricate serious bulk and work on your exhibition in different exercises. Here are other prominent advantages of the rancher's walk you might pass up:
Consumes calories: Like deadlifts and squats, the rancher's walk is a compound. This implies that the activity draws in significant muscle gatherings and a few joints at the same time. Likewise, compound exercises will generally consume a ton of energy, assisting you with consuming a great deal of calories. Likewise, a

rancher's walk is a high-influence work out. This powers your muscles to stay at work longer than required, dissolving additional fat simultaneously. All the more strikingly, this full-body exercise puts your whole body under strain. Subsequently, it constructs bulk in different regions while consuming the additional fat around them, making it a serious, calorie-consuming exercise. In conclusion, a rancher's convey exercise requires steady exertion and concentration since it's typically performed for more than 60 seconds. This extraordinary explosion of movement speeds up the digestion and consumes muscle to fat ratio. Simultaneously, it gets your heart siphoning since it's an extreme focus cardiovascular exercise. **Useful strength:** As well as being a compound exercise, the rancher's convey is likewise a practical activity. Basically, the strength you work while playing out this exercise assists you with undertaking different assignments in your everyday exercises. For example, conveying a bag or packs of basic foods is a genuine variety of the rancher's walk. In this manner, playing out a rancher's stroll in the exercise center will permit you to unhesitatingly embrace such errands more.

Works on cardiovascular wellbeing and perseverance. The rancher's convey is a requesting exercise that will positively make them inhale intensely. In any case, as per research, focused energy exercises like the rancher's convey increment oxygen consuming limit. Thusly, this limits the gamble of cardiovascular circumstances like stroke and coronary episode. Moreover, a rancher's walk gives a few advantages with regards to actual perseverance. This will permit you to support better execution levels for longer. On a similar note, the activity will be trying for your muscles, assisting you with adjusting to the distance and weight as you progress.

Further developed pose: These days, a great many people sit at their work area occupations for over 8 hours every day, prompting expanded instances of terrible stance. Curiously, legitimate activity propensities like doing a rancher's walk are an incredible method for redressing terrible stance. To be exact, a rancher's walk builds your general body and muscle mindfulness by fortifying your center, back, and shoulders. This fundamentally works on your pelvic and spinal arrangement, prompting better stance. Likewise, holding loads in two hands during the activity takes out lopsided characteristics in your body to make soundness. Generally, the activity will lessen weight on your lower and upper back, assisting you with undertaking your everyday errands with better structure.

Assembles bulk quickly: Despite the fact that the rancher's walk is even more a hold rather than a lift, it functions admirably in building bulk. Besides, the activity works the muscle in marginally unexpected ways in comparison to customary strength preparing exercises. This makes it a decent expansion to your exercise program to present variety. Furthermore, the rancher's walk is one of a handful of the activities that challenge all muscle bunches all through the body. This prompts better muscle development in the shoulders, traps, hamstrings, lower arms, glutes, and obliques. In this way, in the event that you're searching for an exercise that will prepare every one of your muscles in a solitary activity, playing out a rancher's stroll at home is a magnificent choice.

Reinforces hold: In the event that you're wanting to embrace any strength preparing, for example, deadlifts, reinforcing your hold first is significant. This is on the grounds that it's beyond difficult to arrive at your maximum capacity with free loads assuming you have powerless grasps. Fortunately, one remarkable advantage of the rancher's walk is that it further develops grasp strength. This is on the grounds that the activity will work your hands, lower arms, back, wrist, and shoulder at the same time. These muscles support your hold strength when they're appropriately prepared. In particular, the exercise will quickly fortify your lower arms, wrists, and hands on account of the tension applied upon them. Plus, you'll push through above lifts and deadlifts without the weight slipping from your hands.

Diminished possibilities of injury. Lifting loads in rancher's convey is a typical practice that we've been accomplishing for quite a long time. For example, our predecessors would convey loads starting with one region then onto the next utilizing their uncovered hands. In spite of the fact that innovation has made things simpler, we actually lift objects in our day to day routines, very much like in rancher's walk. Consequently, our bodies are accustomed to lifting objects here, making it a more normal structure to lift loads. However, more critically, this gamble of injury is very low while doing the rancher's walk, gave you keep up with legitimate structure and concentration while working out.

Rancher's Walk Muscles Worked. One significant advantage of the rancher's walk is that a full-body exercise develops muscle fortitude and perseverance.

Notwithstanding, the activity focuses on certain muscles more intensely than others in view of the idea of the development design. Some significant muscle bunches focused on during a rancher's walk are:

Center: Center muscles are answerable for settling your whole body no matter what the actual activity you're taking part in since they support the pelvis and spine. In any case, it's especially a significant part while you're lifting and conveying weighty burdens. The rancher's walk is really great for fostering a stable areas of strength for and, particularly while utilizing testing loads. This keeps your body steady and upstanding as you stroll forward.

Hip and leg muscles: Strolling while at the same time holding weighty burdens focuses on every one of the muscles in your body. Consequently, the rancher's walk will draw in your glutes, quadriceps, calves, and hamstrings. The hamstrings store mechanical energy when completely extended at the proximal and distal connections before your heel contacts the ground. To put it plainly, they assume a significant part in lifting the legs with each move toward permit sending impetus and settle the knee and hip joints. Like hamstrings, Quads/Quadriceps assume a significant part in knee expansion. This assists with starting the positive headway all through the activity. Then again, the glutes are liable for the hip joint augmentation. Thusly, they're liable for balancing out the hip joint all through your rancher's walk work out. Ultimately, calves are lower leg muscles that assistance to settle the lower leg joint while doing the rancher's walk.

Back: While playing out a rancher's walk, you should keep an inflexible and erect stance to help the heaps on your hands while strolling. This development enacts your upper back muscles, including the snares and trapezius muscles. Likewise, you really want to withdraw your shoulders up and back, assisting you with keeping a tall stance all through the exercise. **Lower arms and Biceps:** The biceps add to hold strength since they're answerable for arm flexion. So when you grasp stacks, these muscles aid somehow. With respect to the rancher's walk, these muscles settle the elbow joint and grasp the load all through the development. Additionally, your lower arms' flexors are intensely connected with while holding and grasping weight. When joined with strolling, this outcomes in staggering hold strength and solid lower arms. Step by step instructions to Do Rancher's Walk The rancher's walk is a suitable exercise for the vast majority and somewhat simple to perform. Notwithstanding, in spite of the straightforwardness of the activity, it's fundamental to guarantee you take care of business. Or probably you might end with injury in the event that you don't do it accurately. Fortunately, in this part, I'll tell you the best way to do a rancher's walk really. Before you start, you will require a few loads to hold in two hands during the exercise. In the event that you're a fledgling, try not to utilize a lot of weight since it is hazardous for you. All things considered, begin with lighter loads and advance gradually until you arrive at a seriously difficult weight.

1. In light of that, follow these moves toward play out a standard rancher's walk.
2. Pick properly weighted free weights and placed them on the floor on every one of your body.

3. Twist down at the knees and hips to arrive at the free weights and handle them in each hand.
4. Hold the hand weights solidly and stand tall while keeping your center, back, and shoulders tight.
5. Step forward and begin strolling reliably, keeping an upstanding stance.
6. Whenever you've arrived at the ideal strolling distance, put the hand weights down while keeping an impartial spine and tight center to stay away from injury.
7. Rest for around 1 to 3 minutes, and rehash the means until you finish the expected sets.

Could You at any point Do a Rancher's Stroll on a Treadmill. In one straightforward word: Yes! Treadmills like Sole F63 Treadmill have demonstrated to be very successful for the individuals who need to play out a lightweight rancher's walk. Nonetheless, there are sure factors you want to remember while doing a rancher's stroll on the treadmill for wellbeing reasons. To begin with, whether or not you're utilizing a collapsing or non-collapsing treadmill, ensure you set the speed at a low setting. Strolling too quick builds your possibilities losing balance and tumbling off the treadmill belt during the activity. Also, likewise with other rancher's walk varieties, keep your center drew in and shoulders down while doing the rancher's carry on the treadmill. This will likewise assist you with keeping up with appropriate structure and stay away from injury. Finally, take more limited steps than you would while strolling on level ground. This will keep you from stumbling off the belt and assist you with keeping your equilibrium while strolling on the hardware. The most effective method to Do A Slope Treadmill Rancher's Walk Turn on the treadmill and set the rhythm at 2 to 3 mph and grade at 15%. Get 20kg weight plates or free weights in two hands and get on the treadmill. Stroll with the free weights at your sides for a specific distance/length, keeping your chest upstanding and center tight.

Rancher's Stroll on Treadmill Wellbeing Contemplations. For the most part, the rancher's walk is viewed as a protected activity for everybody, particularly since you can change time or distance and change the opposition. For example, you can scale the distance strolled and the loads. Be that as it may, there are some security contemplations you ought to remember, particularly if you need to figure out how to do the rancher's stroll on a treadmill. To begin with, in the event that you have a physical issue, try not to do this activity until you've recuperated completely to forestall further injury. Likewise, assuming you have a previous medical issue that restricts your capacity to hit the treadmill, counsel your primary care physician first before you attempt this activity. At long last, the rancher's walk can demolish different medical issue like torment related issues in the lower back, neck, and shoulders. Furthermore, guarantee you keep up with appropriate structure during the activity to stay away from injury and increment the viability of the activity program. This incorporates keeping your spine unbiased during the activity to stay away from lower back wounds. Also, give close consideration to your body during the exercise. Assuming that you experience torment or uneasiness, stop the activity right away and rest for around 2 - 5 minutes prior to continuing the rancher's walk.

In conclusion, consistently pick a weight that gives you full body control through the rancher's convey. In particular, begin the development with lighter loads (10-15lbs.) and stroll for more limited distances (10 - 20 yards) to forestall injury. When the activity begins feeling because of created perseverance, gradually increment the loads you convey and the distance you walk.
End: Rancher's convey basically alludes to strolling while at the same time conveying loads like iron weights or hand weights in your grasp. This practical move offers a few advantages, for example, improving cardio perseverance and reinforcing your center, legs, and back chain. Even better, you can change the force of the activity by utilizing heavier or lighter loads, and you could do the rancher's stroll on a treadmill. Additionally, consolidate legitimate nourishment, warm-ups and rest into your daily practice to see nonstop improvement with this activity.

Habitually Sought clarification on some pressing questions.
1.Question How long to do the rancher's walk?
You can play out your rancher's stroll for 25 - 30 seconds or walk 10 steps in the right direction and back. Do this for 2 to 3 sets, keeping up with legitimate structure and procedure all through each set.

2.QUESTION How much weight for a rancher's walk do I want?
Rancher's walk is a straightforward and safe activity that helps gain strong perseverance and strength. Even better, it permits you to try different things with different loads. As a novice, you ought to begin with 25 lbs on each hand and bit by bit increment the load as your

grasp strength increments. Then again, high level lifters can convey their complete body weight for north of 30 seconds.

3.QUESTION How frequently would it be a good idea for one to do a rancher's walk? Since the rancher's convey isn't so requesting as the deadlift, you can do it at least a time or two every week. For the most part, doing the rancher's walk 1 to 3 times each week is an extraordinary objective, yet that will rely upon your exercise plan.

4.QUESTION Is rancher's walk a decent cardio exercise? Rancher's walk has demonstrated to be an astounding type of cardiovascular exercise. To be exact, the additional obstruction expands your pulse and assists with building slender bulk.

CHAPTER 3……………….BEST TREADMILL FOR Youngsters

In view of security concerns, the absence of enough jungle gyms, and the ongoing pandemic, most children remain inside. Sadly, this frequently causes well being concerns like stoutness. Luckily, a children treadmill will make a great activity instrument for your kids to remain dynamic and construct sound activity propensities. Need assistance tracking down the best treadmills for youngsters.

Initially Best like.

1. Redmon Children Treadmill.
2. Redmon Air Walker.
3. RIYIFER Non-mechanized Home Treadmill.
4. YHKJ Youngsters Treadmill.
5. Fitnex XT5
6. Redmon multi-capability rower.
7. Hey!Play! Toy Seat and Leg Press.

The children's treadmills on this rundown have been cautiously handpicked in view of value, solidness, and security. To find out more, continue to peruse.

1. Redmon Children Treadmill

Highlights

Froth wrapped metal tubing

No-tip plan

Electronic screen

Non-mechanized.

In the event that you're looking for a protected treadmill for youngsters, this self move treadmill from Redmon merits considering. It marks each container with regards to being the most solid and secure activity piece of hardware for youngsters. The Redmon Children Treadmill is about safe exercise meetings for your little one. The no-tip plan, for example, guarantees that any youngster that desires to run or stroll on a treadmill will actually want to do so securely. It even accompanies an electronic screen, which you can use for time-slip by that consequently switches off following 10 minutes. What's more, it's a self-impel treadmill, so there's less opportunity of your children stumbling and falling or harming their fingers due to the moving parts. Besides, the Redmon treadmill includes a froth covering for extra security on every one of the metal cylinders. Additionally, setting up the treadmill is quite simple since you get every one of the instruments fundamental for collecting it. As per the organization, this exercise machine is reasonable for 3-6-year-old children and has a client weight breaking point of 100 lbs. In any case, a few kids might battle to move the treadmill's belt. Thus, it could require your youngster a little investment to become acclimated to this wellness machine. Furthermore, a few guardians had issues about the belt not continuously remaining set up. Additionally, you'll need to buy the battery independently for the electronic screen. **Aces:** No-tip configuration implies more secure and more dependable for your child, with an electronic screen, you can set time-slip by and even utilize auto-off metal cylinders highlight froth wraps to guarantee well being. **Cons:** No batteries included.

2.Redmon Air Walker

Highlights

Non-mechanized

No-tip plan

Tough development.

If you have any desire to get the best gift for a five-year-old kid, you can't turn out badly with this air walker by Redmon. Besides, it's a tomfoolery and cool-looking wellness gadget to keep your kid dynamic. Security is the principal thing on each parent's brain while getting a children's treadmill. With the Redmon Air Walker, you can reassure you realizing it sports a protected plan. Take the no-tip include, for instance. It makes the gadget protected and solid. With Redmon Air Walker, your kid can hold their well being under wraps with a tomfoolery, non-influence exercise. It's likewise non-mechanized, and that implies your child has unlimited authority over the machine's speed. This likewise means less possibility of injury from a fall brought about by the moving parts. This air walker likewise flaunts a strong casing, because of the powder-covered steel. Also, the froth wrapped metal cylinders and hostile to slip surface assist with limiting injury gambles. At last, similar to the Redmon treadmill, it's quite simple to gather. You get every one of

the instruments and a client manual that makes the entire arrangement process consistent and simple. While the Redmon air walker would make an incredible gift for youngsters matured 3-6, you should search for another treadmill in the event that your kid is more seasoned. Like all self-push treadmills, this one requires a slight expectation to learn and adapt.
Aces: Hostile to slide surface keeps your child from falling, No-tip plan and the non-mechanized framework make the walker protected and solid, Simple to put together, Sturdy development to endure your child's harsh use.
Cons: Not great for youngsters more established than six years

3.RIYIFER Non-Mechanized Home Treadmill
Highlights

Electronic screen

Delicate froth covering

Simple to utilize

Hostile to slip pedals.
If cash isn't an issue and you need to offer your child the best activity machine, then the RYIFER non-mechanized home treadmill is your response. It has all that you'll normally track down in the top of the line youngster's treadmill. From hostile to slip pedals to an electronic screen to delicate froth metal covers and a solid casing, the RYIFER got you covered. Unmistakably intended for 3-6-year-old children, this non-mechanized treadmill furnishes your kid with a great method for meeting their everyday portion of active work. Its finished enemy of slide surface guarantees your kid will encounter a charming low-serious treadmill exercise. The sidebars and handles

highlight a froth covering for added insurance against injury. The treadmill even accompanies an electric screen for recording exercise information. It utilizes 2 AA batteries to drive up the screen, which naturally switches off following ten minutes. Generally speaking, the RYIFER treadmill can assist with working on your child's equilibrium and impart day to day practice propensities in them. Collecting the gadget is a breeze. You get every one of the devices you'll require and a guidance manual to make the treadmill ready in a brief time frame. The main disadvantage with this machine is its robust sticker price.

Aces: Electric screen to record practice information, Sidebars and handles have delicate froth covers for added assurance, Hostile to slip pedals forestall fall.

Cons: Really costly.

4.YHKJ Kids Treadmill
Highlights

Manual treadmill

Simple establishment process

Froth wrapped metal design

Screen.

The YHKJ Youngsters Treadmill is one more fantastic choice for youngsters matured 4-10. With this exercise machine at home, you won't stress over your kid's absence of open air exercises. The counter slip pedals on this treadmill increment erosion, which helps give kids a reasonable activity experience and furthermore keeps them from falling. Obliging a greatest load of 150 lbs is likewise sufficient. With froth wrappings across the sidebars and handles, this treadmill offers a delicate touch and safeguards your child during exercise. Moreover, it accompanies a screen that shows mileage. As a non-electric treadmill, your kid will decide the treadmill's speed, making it a lot more secure. Also, its brilliant, fun varieties will additionally persuade and get your kid eager to work out. The treadmill is likewise moderately lightweight, so you can rapidly move it starting with one room then onto the next according to your kid's inclination. It's likewise simple to assemble. Be that as it may, more youthful children might think that it is excessively exceptional.

Aces: Masters Delicate padded sidebars and handles, No-slip surface, Advanced screen, Simple arrangement process.

Cons: It could call for a little investment for more youthful children to utilize it.

5. Fitnex XT5

Highlights

Bottle holder

Mechanized

Height changing choice

4 activity modes. Any parent searching for a quality treadmill for more seasoned kids ought to think about the Fitnex XT5. In numerous ways, the XT5 is essentially similar to a grown-up treadmill. Nonetheless, it has a few high level elements that urge more seasoned children to practice more. You get numerous modes for various activities, including fat consume, cardio, span, and perseverance. Furthermore, it has advanced counters to show pulse, calories, distance, speed, and LAPS. The XT5 accompanies a two-drive machine bragging a greatest speed 0.5 mph. You might tweak the height on the off

chance that you wish. Additionally, there are seven criticism choices. With a container holder set up, your youngster can work out and remain hydrated without moving around a lot to get water. Yet, remember that it's not reasonable for more youthful children. Generally, the XT5 is a vigorous treadmill with a few inventive highlights. Additionally, being mechanized, it's fundamental to try not to allow children to utilize the treadmill without you around.

Aces: Numerous practicing modes, Jug holder, Seven input choices ,Drove show to check the time, pulse, and distance.

Cons: Not great for solo utilization

6.Redmon Multi-capability Rower

Highlights

Durable development

Protected and solid

Compact.

For the individuals who need to get their children a tomfoolery, multi-capability wellness machine, the Redmon Multi-capability Rower merits considering. It's solid, dependable, safe, and offers a tomfoolery, less-influence exercise insight. The Redmon Multi-capability Rower flaunts rock solid development, requiring almost no support. Also, it will be sufficiently able to deal with your youngster's unpleasant use. In the event that you're reluctant to get a treadmill for your kid, this will make a superb other option. Furthermore, it looks pretty like the standard paddling machine that you'll find at the rec center. This one has been planned unequivocally for 3-6-year-old youngsters. With its splendid, popping tones, this rower will assist you with advancing a solid

propensity for practicing day to day to your children. Furthermore, it's lightweight, making it a compact children's activity machine. Also, it's non-mechanized, so your child can practice as indicated by their own favored speed. The main issue with this wellness hardware for youngsters is that the paint might fall off after some utilization. **Aces:** Professionals Substantial development and requires less upkeep, Ideal for 3 to 6-year-old children, It's very versatile, Safe practicing machine for youngsters.
Cons: Paint will in general fall off after some utilization

7.Hey!Play! Toy Seat and Leg Press
Highlights

Sturdy materials

Lightweight loads

Instructive and fun exercise kids toy

Froth wrapped outline. The Toy Seat and Leg Press from Hello! Play! is one of the most mind-blowing toys for young men that you can get today. This exercise machine will permit you to teach kids about legitimate weightlifting structures. In addition, you can show them how muscles work while performing leg or seat press on it. This exercise gear flaunts a solid material development. Its seat and hand weight outline are made utilizing sturdy, powder-covered steel. Accordingly, the whole unit is sufficiently able to endure customary use in your children's den. The edge and free weight toy include a delicate froth covering. This offers appropriate padding when your child does his leg or seat press works out. What's more, the removable loads are lightweight and won't cause strain or injury.

You can likewise change the free weight rack, permitting it to serve your kid longer as they keep on developing. In any case, it has a most extreme weight breaking point of 150 lbs. On the disadvantage, it very well may be excessively little for youngsters who are 6-years and more established.
Aces: Strong development for enduring use, Froth covered free weight and casing offer legitimate padding any place required , Lightweight loads to forestall injury or strain. **Cons:** Not Great for more established kids

How We Picked the Best Children Treadmills As you may have guessed! We didn't simply pick the items arbitrarily. Prior to making this rundown, it was considered a couple of rules, which include:
1.Highlights: Items with helpful highlights are more functional than those with bounty, which you won't actually require. We separated and reduced the items for this rundown in light of that.
2.Particulars: You can constantly gauge the item's quality quantitatively with numbers. While we picked treadmills that brag higher details, we guaranteed it was of the right equilibrium.
3. Brand esteem: It's not shrewd to go for less-known brands since they offer items at a lower cost. In the event that you do, your possibilities getting a bad quality item get higher. Likewise, recollect that famous brands will constantly attempt to keep up with their standing, in contrast to other people. Top youngsters' electric treadmill brands offer extraordinary highlights to isolate their items from others. Consequently, you'll ideally find a couple of ideal treadmills for your child on this rundown.
4.Client audits and evaluations: This is another essential standard

we thought about while making our rundown. Items with better evaluations mean a respectable number of clients experienced better help. Likewise, client surveys assist you with acquiring important and genuine criticism about the children's treadmills from certifiable clients. **5. An incentive for cash:** Indeed, a modest item isn't great 100% of the time. Yet, nor is following through on a weighty cost on ostentatious yet low quality items. So we ensured we just picked treadmills for youngsters that offer nice incentive for cash. Instructions to Purchase a Treadmill for Youngsters Teaching great activity propensities in your kids will assist with keeping them fit and looking great. Particularly taking into account the ascent of weight in kids, remaining dynamic is fundamental for your young ones. A children treadmill is a superb exercise device for the people who invest a large portion of their energy inside. Be that as it may, how to recognize the best? You can do as such by thinking about the accompanying pointers. Well being Highlights You can't miss this part while picking the right treadmill for your child. Ensure the one you pick has the accompanying well being highlights:

1. Side rails: At the point when even grown-ups in some cases find it hard to stay aware of the machine's speed, it's workable for a youngster to excursion and fall while running on the treadmill. Thusly, pick one that elements side rails as they can assist them with keeping up with balance, especially when they're depleted. Likewise, check whether the side rails have a froth covering as it forestalls calluses and is more secure for kids.

2.Sturdiness: Since it's a child treadmill doesn't mean it'll be modest. You ought to put resources into a strong treadmill, ideally one that can endure longer than your child's advantage in work out.

Also, kids are less inclined to ponder the machine's upkeep. Thus, the one you get ought to be adequately solid to endure the children's harsh use.

3. Space: While overlay capable treadmills are perfect for little spaces, finding a fordable choice for kids is really phenomenal. Consequently, you need to consider the treadmill aspects and check whether your house is adequately roomy to oblige it. Furthermore, guardians with more youthful youngsters ought to get the treadmill far from other activity machines to limit mishap chances.

4. Strength: Regardless of whether you're getting an electric treadmill, your child will be running and strolling on it. You don't need an unsound machine that can spill when your kid rests on one side. Subsequently, it's ideal to get one stable enough to oblige your child's weight without spilling.

Mechanized or Non-mechanized. One continuous discussion among guardians while picking a treadmill for their kids is whether to get a non-mechanized or mechanized treadmill. Here are our opinion on this. Assume you pick a non-mechanized model like the one from RIYEFER. Your kid will push the treadmill's belt while strolling or running on this treadmill. What's more, since they control the machine's speed, they will not need to stress over keeping up the speed. Besides, such models need programmed moving parts, which can hurt your little one coincidentally. In any case, note that non-mechanized treadmills have a greatest client weight cutoff of <100 lbs, making them ideal for more youthful children. Mechanized treadmills, running against the norm, are more qualified for greater children. That is on the grounds that they're better at adjusting themselves and can match the

speed of the machine's belts. This choice additionally has more elements to keep the youngsters propelled to work out. You could try and have the option to coordinate a treadmill application for novices with such machines.
Significant Note: Never leave your youngster unaided on a mechanized treadmill. Purchasers Guide: Fast Rundown No opportunity to peruse the whole piece? Here is a fast outline to assist you with picking: Need Treadmills with Screens? Pretty much every item on this accompanies a screen. Redmon Children treadmill, RIYIFER Non-mechanized Home Treadmill, and YHKJ Kids Treadmill have comparative screens. However, in the event that you need a further developed show, the XT5 merits considering. Do take note of that it's just great for more seasoned kids. Need a solid children treadmill? While every one of the treadmills on this rundown gloat a durable form, the one from RYIFER takes the top position. Searching for elective exercise hardware for youngsters? Redmon multi-capability rower and Hey!Play! Toy Seat and Leg Press are two extraordinary other options and will assist with keeping your children dynamic and impart sound activity propensities.

Habitually Sought clarification on some pressing questions. This part will address the most consuming inquiries guardians have while buying treadmills for their children. Along these lines, continue to peruse to find out more.

1.Question How does a children's treadmill function?
Treadmills for youngsters are intended to permit them to securely get

their normal portion of activity. You'll generally find the non-mechanized choices as it's more secure for youngsters contrasted with electric treadmills. In children's treadmills, the kid needs to involve their feet for the belt to move. Accordingly, your children are less inclined to fall and harm themselves.

2.Question How old should a youngster be to utilize a treadmill?
For the most part, your youngster should associate with 12-13 years of age to utilize treadmills. Notwithstanding, the rules might fluctuate starting with one producer then onto the next. In this manner, you ought to go through the treadmill client manual to figure out which age bunch it suggests. In the event that your kid is under 12 years of age and there could be no alternate method for playing outside, they can utilize a children's treadmill under oversight. Non-mechanized treadmills are planned only for youngsters and consent to kid security principles. This rendition of treadmills is likewise fitting for youngsters matured 3-7. Be that as it may, sure, you really want to save your eyes on them however long they're on the treadmill.

3.Question Is a treadmill OK for youngsters? By and large, it's not suggested that your kid utilize a treadmill, particularly in the event that they're youthful. Luckily, a few presumed brands offer treadmills that are OK for kids. Notwithstanding, you ought to never allow your child to utilize this exercise machine unattended to stay away from injury gambles. You can additionally guarantee your little's one's well being by following security measures and ensuring they're wearing legitimate running shoes and a children's running coat.

4.Question For what reason is the Peloton Tread+ Perilous for Little Children and Creatures?
Peloton tread+ flaunts a strong engine and a brace belt, which could demonstrate deadly for little children and creatures. What's more, when the treadmill's supports roll under the deck, a hole structures at the track's end; this represents a significant danger since little items are defenseless to being trapped in the opening and pulled under (This was the situation in the Peloton treadmill child passing).
End: In this way, these are the absolute best treadmills for youngsters Every item on this rundown offers something exceptional and is reasonable for various age gatherings. Thu sly, the right treadmill for your child will eventually rely upon your youngster's age, inclination, and spending plan. Whichever item you pick, ensure you follow appropriate security gauges and try not to leave your children unaided. You can make it more secure for your kids to practice on the treadmill by getting them a couple of value running shoes. Look at this article on the Adidas running shoes for babies for motivation.

CHAPTER 4............TREADMILL Exercises FOR Greater BUTT Best Exercise

Albeit the vast majority need to get more fit, a few ladies need a more modest midsection and enormous goods. As a rule, the size of your butt is impacted by hereditary qualities. Nonetheless, you can likewise foster huge goods on the treadmill by performing exercises that focus on your glutes. Over the long haul, this will prompt a more tight tush, making your butt look appealing.

However, what are a portion of these activities that can assist with conditioning and shape your butt? Indeed, that is the very thing that I'll be checking here out. In this way, read on to find the best exercises to assist you with developing large goods on a treadmill.

What Muscles Does the Treadmill Attempt to Fabricate a Greater Butt.

Glutes are the muscles answerable for molding the bottom. In particular, there are 3 sorts of gluteal muscle gatherings; gluteus minimus, medius and maximus. As the name 'maximus' infers, the gluteus maximus is the most noticeable and greatest muscle gathering of the butt. In addition, it's the biggest and most grounded muscle in the body. In any case, gluteus minimus and medius ought not be neglected since they guarantee pelvic solidness. This will keep you from encountering leg torment in the wake of showing on the treadmill to keeping you liberated from injury and assisting you with keeping up with great structure while working out. Likewise, all gluteal muscles contain a combination of quick jerk and slow-jerk strands. Commonly, quick jerk filaments create when tested with eruptions of speed, while slow-jerk strands foster through perseverance works out, including uphill running.

How Does the Treadmill Assemble Your Glutes. Running and strolling on a treadmill helps fabricate your glutes by lessening fat around there while expanding and conditioning its bulk. Preparing at a high slope level is most useful while utilizing the machine to address glutes since it results in a critical and alluring body. Besides, a treadmill permits you to detach and target muscles that can assist you with getting a greater butt. In particular, running and strolling on the machine works the glutes, giving you a more tight, more adjusted look. As per a recent report, there are no massive contrasts in the biometrics of open air and treadmill running. Hence, treadmill preparing will actuate your glutes and hamstrings as much as running outside. Far better, treadmills are furnished with a slope component to assist you with developing your posterior. Raising the grade gives a phenomenal obstruction and powers you to connect with the center and lower body, bringing about greater rump over the long run. Advantages of Utilizing Treadmill to Foster Greater Backside The treadmill may not seem like the most superb way to deal with reinforce and condition your glutes. Nonetheless, it gives a few treadmill advantages to the rear end and different muscles like hamstrings. Likewise, you can utilize the machine for cardio exercises, which are great for consuming calories, keeping up with the soundness of your organ frameworks, and expanding perseverance. These angles are significant in your butt-building exercise as you expect to reshape and solidify your glutes.

**Best Treadmill Exercises for Glutes.
Vital Treadmill strolling:** The first treadmill exercise that will assist with chiseling your glutes is utilized for strolling lurches. To begin: Increment the grade to 15% and diminish the speed of the moving belt to ⅔ miles each hour. Make one long stride advances and twist into the front. Rehash this cycle with your other leg and continue onward for around 2 - 3 minutes to heat up or chill off. On the other hand, pivot on the machine and walk in reverse. At the same time, increment the grade to 8 - 15% and diminish the speed to 2 miles each hour. All the more significantly, ensure you hold the handrails while pivoting and strolling in reverse to focus on your gluteal muscles from an alternate point. Ultimately, stroll for around 5 min to chill off from the runs or slopes.
Treadmill running: Running is an incredible activity for your bum since it consumes fat and fabricates muscles. Despite the fact that treadmill running will develop glutes as much as fortitude preparation, it's very powerful. Like some other type of running, playing out this exercise on a treadmill centers around 2 kinds of muscle fiber; Slow-jerk (Type 1) and quick jerk (Type 2). As referenced before, quick jerk strands assist strong butts with delivering abrupt energy blasts during runs. Going against the norm, slow-jerk filaments foster tones butts that advance perseverance

running like long distance races and 5K races. **Slope/Grade preparing for glutes:** The initial step of making your treadmill preparing add to greater rear end is raising the grade. Scientists even led a review distributed in 2007 in the 'Diary of Trial Science to look at the job of the gluteus maximus in strolling and running. The review laid out that this muscle is more dynamic while climbing or running up a precarious slope. In addition, treadmill slant benefits abs and help to tone leg muscles. Running on a treadmill at least 12% grade will assist you with receiving the treadmill rewards for glutes given by the machine.

This is the way to play out a slope preparing for the butts on the treadmill: Run or stroll for 5 - 10 min at an agreeable 1% grade to heat up. Elective 1 moment of quick strolling or running at a 5 - 15% slope with brief level surface running. Keep rotating level streets and slopes for around 30 - 40 min until you complete the activity. Besides, ensure you hit the treadmill surfaces with your heels first while doing the slope to draw in the glutes.

Run exercise: A short, strong run treadmill is an extraordinary method for supplementing your endeavors to fabricate a greater butt with power lifting.

How Does Running Form Glutes: Straightforward! Running purposes quick jerk (type 2) muscles that rapidly use a ton of energy. These strands are bigger and initiate when there are unexpected eruptions of development. Additionally, they've less veins since they don't expect oxygen to keep up with the short explosions of oxygen.

This makes running an 'anaerobic' exercise, very much like strength preparing. On similar note, type 2 filaments increment muscle size, so running will support the goods. To initiate those quick jerk muscles and assist with building your rear, play out the accompanying run exercises a couple of times each week: Begin with a light run or quick stroll for 5 - 10 minutes to heat up. With your treadmill slant at 0%, run at your quickest speed for 30 seconds. Dial back your speed and stroll for 1 to 2 minutes to recuperate. Shift back and forth between 30-sec runs and 1 brief recuperation meetings 10 to multiple times.

Intense cardio exercise (HIIT): In spite of the fact that HIIT is testing, it's one of the best butts conditioning treadmill exercises. Rather than strolling quicker, this sort of treadmill exercise includes expanding the power by raising the slope. In addition, it consolidates cardiovascular activity with strength preparing. Subsequently, it will support your digestion, consume calories and work your butt muscles. Prior to playing out this exercise, warm up on your treadmill for 5 minutes at a speed of 2.5 to 3.5 mph. Then, gradually speed up and lean to suit your wellness level. For instance, you can speed up to 4.5 - 6 mph and run for 1 moment. Also, keep substituting spans for the whole exercise. All the more significantly, twist the knees a little during the serious exercise stages to work the glutes. Glute enactment treadmill strolling rushes Performing rushes off or on the treadmill is a viable method for conditioning your butt. Simultaneously, strolling rushes will straighten out your things and glutes. Sadly, strolling jumps need space to walk, however space is generally restricted, particularly at home. This is where having a treadmill proves to be useful! By setting the machine to the ideal speed, you can consummate this treadmill exercise for glutes over the long haul to make a normal that will assist you with fostering a jiggly goods strolling. To summarize, doing thrusts on the treadmill will keep you strolling relentless, thus enacting your glute muscles beginning to end. The glute muscle initiation will assist you with developing greater glutes. Also, consolidating rushes in your treadmill exercise will assist you with forestalling weariness while conditioning and lifting your tush. On a similar note, you can utilize thrusts to transform your exercise into a circuit work-out daily schedule. To accomplish this, switch back and forth between 3 minutes of treadmill running, running or strolling with 45 seconds of treadmill strolling jumps for the whole exercise. Notwithstanding, while at the same time doing the strolling rushes, lessen the treadmill speed to a sluggish speed of 2.5 - 3mph for wellbeing reasons. This is additionally fundamental while running during pregnancy's most memorable trimester on the treadmill since it will keep you from harming yourself or tumbling off the moving belt.

End: Treadmill preparing is a key activity that can assist you with building greater bum. The exercises target type 1 and type 2 muscle filaments that foster butt muscles. Thus, assuming you are hoping to tighten up your glutes and develop huge goods on the treadmill, the exercises we've recorded above will assist you with that. Be that as it may, coordinate these treadmill exercises with other butt-conditioning exercises like squats, hip pivots, and lurches. Likewise, guarantee your exercises are joined by a sound eating routine comprising of low-fat dairy, entire grains, lean proteins, and adequate green vegetables.

Habitually Sought clarification on some pressing questions.
1.QUESTION Does the treadmill make your bum more modest?
Preparing on a treadmill might make your bum more modest by diminishing fat around there. Be that as it may, treadmill exercises help to shape and tone your butts by expanding the bulk of your glutes, particularly while strolling on the machine utilizing a high slope.

2.QUESTION Does the treadmill make your legs greater?
Treadmill preparing doesn't make your legs become bigger. All things being equal, treadmill strolling or running reinforces your leg muscles and further develops muscle perseverance.

3.QUESTION Is treadmill preparing great for the bottom?
Running or strolling on a treadmill is an incredible method for conditioning your butt, assisting you with creating more tight and lifted bottom. Additionally, the wellness gear helps your hamstrings, glutes, and quadriceps cooperate to guarantee they're conditioned during the exercise.

4.QUESTION How would I cause my bum to get greater quick?
If you have any desire to make your bum greater, do cardio exercises that focus on your glutes and butt-developing fortitude preparation practices 3 times each week. Additionally, change your eating routine to help your butt-building objective.

CHAPTER 5.........TREADMILL
Exercise For Soccer Players

Assuming there is anything that soccer players respect so a lot, it is that they can keep an elevated degree of cardiovascular wellness, which can support them generally through the hour and a half of serious activity on the pitch. Curiously, to accomplish this, numerous soccer players have recognized treadmill exercise as a cheat sheet to stay in shape and remain in structure during instructional courses and in any event, during the primary test. You might inquire, "does the Soccer exercise work?" Assuming that is your inquiry, the straightforward response is indeed, the different Soccer exercise cardio routine is a go-to wellness routine with numerous succulent advantages for soccer players. In this way, the soccer treadmill exercise will give you a delicate landing when you really want to construct the bulk to assist you with beating your rival and crush the ball past the goalkeeper.

What is the Soccer Exercise: The Soccer treadmill exercise ought not be absent from your regular exercise routine timetable. Indeed, with next to no goal to exhaust you with numerous accounts, the Soccer running exercise or Soccer preparing are basic activities to do at home, particularly when you include the treadmill gear inside the solace of your home. With these activities, it is feasible to provide your body with an everyday portion of the Soccer diet for that bulk, endurance, running velocity, and spryness you really want to move the ball past your rival gracefully.

4 Soccer Treadmill Exercise for Soccer Players. In the event that you want to put yourself through the Soccer wellness test or basically need to participate in various Soccer HIIT exercises, here are the absolute best soccer treadmill exercises each and every other soccer player utilizations to remain in front of their game. Maybe you don't have the advantage of possessing a piece of a treadmill and other exercise center hardware in your home; there are a modest bunch of stores you can lease rec center gear for home.

1.Fartlek Preparing: Soccer players don't necessarily move at a similar speed or in a similar bearing. Nonetheless, players should rapidly change from strolling to a quick running, cutting slantingly, and, surprisingly, going in reverse because of the idea of the game. Thus, a treadmill Fartlek running project is one of the Soccer HIIT exercises to plan for this occasion. Strangely, this is a kind of span preparing in which you walk, run, or run for shifting measures of time. While doing this, you can cycle between strolling, running, and running aimlessly stretches utilizing the treadmill's speed buttons. Fartlek Treadmill Exercise Test Despite the fact that fartlek preparing has all the earmarks of being a helpful choice for those people who aren't prepared to challenge themselves, don't befuddle "unstructured" with "inadvertent." In this way, prior to beginning Soccer preparing, set a speed or term plan for you and begin any fartlek exercise. Notwithstanding, while at the same time doing this, guarantee that you have a procedure for controlling the speed increase or tension. By the by, the time length and rates are the most appropriate for experienced sprinters and soccer players, however you can change the velocities to suit your capacity. **The following are the moves toward start your fartlek treadmill exercise.**

Warm up by tenderly running or strolling for a normal of around 6-7 minutes at 3.0 miles each hour. While doing this, guarantee that you set the slope to around 7%. Then, at that point, at a 1 percent tendency, run for a normal of 2 miles at 12mph. Require a three-minute separate by easing back to five miles each hour, and while doing as such, don't change the slope. Advance to 6.5 mph for 30 seconds for the exercise set. Play out an additional three-minute rest and go on at around 5-6 mph. Continue onward going on like this and expanding for 30-35 seconds prior to diminishing for 3-4 minutes. proceed with this until it's around 20 minutes. Move forward your running velocity to around 6-7 miles each hour and run another mile. Wrap up by a sluggish running at 3.3 mph on a 6-7% slope briefly of unwinding. Wrap up with a couple extends whenever you are finished unwinding. Thus, assuming you need your name written in gold in the astounding universe of soccer, the John Terry treadmill exercise ought not be absent from your consistent exercise schedule plan.

2. Slant running: Soccer's exercise incorporates straightforward slope running and stays one of the surest procedures to improve your leg strength. When you utilize a treadmill with the grade set at around 12% or above, you can partake in the delicious advantages connected to uphill running even from the solace of your home. Obviously, this is likewise awesome assuming your house is found where there is no slope. You can attempt span preparing with different slope rates to have a decent exercise blend.

Treadmill Grade Rules and Tips To begin. It is great to get ready for a normal of 5-6 minutes utilizing a slight slope or level strolling at an exceptionally sluggish speed. Whenever that is finished, you can embrace these moves toward get more bangs for your treadmill work out.

a. Comprehend how your treadmill hardware functions By and large, most treadmill gear permits you to change the grade in any event, during your exercise, though you can make such acclimations to others before your exercise meeting. This infers that at pretty much every point, you should change the slope of your treadmill. This, you can tell, is certainly not a smart thought, particularly while completing stretch exercises.

b. Utilize the right treadmill strategies When your grade level has expanded, making great stance with more limited strides is fitting. For instance, don't incline in reverse; all things considered, propel yourself forward. Attempt as must as conceivable to overlook your handrails. The normal outcomes won't come when you can't relinquish the handrails. In a circumstance where you are OK with strolling steps, utilize a decent tough working step.

c. Changes ought to be done step by step It is normal to move at a more slow speed while going uphill, which will be reflected in your breathing and pulse since they will show that your body is in for a requesting walk. Thus, it is vital to permit this to screen how well you've gone with your exercise rather than your speed. Notwithstanding, it might be ideal assuming you comprehended that any treadmill's exercise power is an element of speed, slope, and span. In this way, assuming you decide to make your slope more extreme, guarantee that you cut down your speed and time. With this, you can continuously speed up and time as you ace a more extreme slope.

3. Runs: Similarly as with other running classifications, runs work on your cardiovascular organ's wellness, particularly for soccer players. Running is additionally an activity that can reinforce your legs and fabricate your gathering of muscles. Regularly, runs help to fabricate the muscle fiber of your hamstrings and quadriceps, and it assists you with moving the ball past your rival effortlessly. It is exhorted that you spend the initial couple of moments gradually changing your speed from a walk around a fast run, and from that point forward, switch between two minutes of running at maximum velocity and strolling, individually.

The following are a moves toward get the best while running with a treadmill.

Stage 1: The principal thing to do is to fire up the machine. Whenever it's begun, get on it and begin with a sluggish speed. Before long, you'll find that it's very much like going for a lively stroll. Do this for a couple of moments.

Stage 2: Gradually increment the speed on the treadmill until you've broken into a run. Do this for a couple of moments.

Stage 3: Dial back the speed/pace of the treadmill to a walk and enjoy some time off.

Stage 4: Proceed with exercise by expanding the speed of the treadmill back to a run, and do it for some time.

Stage 5: Take part in the run again and again for a couple of additional minutes. Attempt to stretch your boundary.

Stage 6: Return the treadmill speed to a walk and have some time off for a couple of moments.

Running utilizing the treadmill machine The above is only an illustration of a run exercise you might participate in. Assuming running is different to you, I exhort that you start with a 10-second run at spans until you are fit. Supportive alerts while running utilizing the treadmill machine Guarantee to run at an agreeable speed, don't attempt to exhaust yourself, particularly on the off chance that you are new to running. Running is an exercise that requests a ton from you. Assuming working out is different to you, guarantee that you counsel your PCP prior to beginning another gym routine daily practice.

4. In reverse and sideways running: Without a doubt, it will not be letting it be known that sideways and in reverse development is one of the familiar headings soccer players move in when on the pitch. Anyway, how would you foster your endurance and assemble your mobility to head through these paths without breaking down even before the primary portion of the match? The response is pretty much as basic as utilizing the treadmill gear to mimic the different headings you will perhaps be heading through during a match. While on your treadmill, make a few time for in reverse and sideways running as opposed to involving the entire exercise meeting for running forward.

Tips for sideways and in reverse running on a treadmill. Utilize these treadmill running tips to benefit from your experience on the machine. Warm up It's enticing to step on your treadmill and start your standard exercise just. Be that as it may, as other outside practices like running and running, you should have a concise snapshot of warm-up prior to diving deep into the extreme piece of your exercise routine daily schedule. In the event you might be pondering, heating up is an effective method for moving forward the pulse, get adequate oxygen to your muscle, and increment your internal heat level. These, all aspects of your body will be really proficient.

Grasp the working of your treadmill gear Gain proficiency with the different elements of your gear to capitalize on your exercise. In the event that you're utilizing a treadmill at the rec center, request that a coach tell you the best way to utilize it before you get on the grounds that it's not generally clear from the beginning. Numerous treadmills accompany: A heart screen, Speed show, A calories consume mini-computer, Pre-set exercises.

Utilize a slight slope: Change the treadmill's grade to somewhere in the range of 1% and 2%. Obviously, on the off chance that you're starting to begin running, it's fine to leave your treadmill's grade at zero until you've worked on your wellness and acquired treadmill solace. In any case, don't unwind whenever you've become accustomed to it in light of the fact that keeping a zero grade is comparable to running on a little downhill. All things considered, for to some degree a piece of your exercise, have a go at raising your speed or slope so you feel tested.

Try not to make it excessively steep: At the same time, don't steep the grade excessively (surpassing 7%); this will mount superfluous burden on your lower legs, hips, and back. A few sprinters accept they are getting great activity on the off chance that they endeavor to run the whole distance on a precarious slope (anything more than 2%).

Try not to clutch the handrail: Certain individuals accept they should clutch the handrails while strolling or running on a treadmill.

Notwithstanding, the handrails are simply there to help you in securely getting on and off the treadmill.
Try not to incline forward: Keep a straight stance. Since the treadmill dawdles in reverse, you don't have to incline forward. On the off chance that you incline forward excessively far, you take an enormous risk and back torment as well as losing your balance.
Try not to peer down: It's troublesome not to look at the control center to check how long or separate you have left, yet your running structure will endure assuming you do. Likewise, try not to check your feet out. You'll in all probability be stooped over, which could cause back and neck torment.
Try not to step on or while the treadmill is moving: Hopping or tumbling from a quick treadmill is one of the main sources of treadmill wounds. Thus, consistently guarantee that you delayed down the speed of the treadmill hardware prior to stepping on or out of the machine.
End: A treadmill exercise is without a doubt a must-pursue each soccer player who desires to prevail in their profession. With lots of routine wellness exercises that should be possible utilizing a treadmill, run, fartlek preparing, in reverse and sideways running, and slanted running are top on the rundown of treadmill exercises for each soccer player.

Habitually Sought clarification on some pressing questions.
1.Question Is the treadmill a piece of good exercise gear for soccer players?
Without a doubt, a treadmill is the ideal exercise gear each soccer player ought to possess in light of the fact that it is a certain method

for remaining fit and further develop their soccer execution directly in the solace of their homes. With this, they don't be guaranteed to have to go to the exercise center each time they need to chip away at their running velocity and mobility methods.

2.Question Does a treadmill exercise further develop endurance?
A treadmill doesn't just assistance soccer players to consume calories or work on their running pace. All things being equal, it likewise further develops soccer players' endurance, particularly while completing stretch or slope preparing.

3.Question What are a few weaknesses of utilizing a treadmill?
Modern treadmill hardware can be really costly, and their high effect during running can cause serious torments around the joints, lower legs, hips, and even knees.

4.Question What gathering of muscles does a piece of treadmill hardware work?
Albeit basically every one of the muscles in the body are locked in during an instructional course utilizing a treadmill, the most well-known target muscles incorporate the thighs, hamstrings, quadriceps, glutes, and calves. Nonetheless, with a more extreme slope, different muscles, like the muscular strength, are likewise drawn in with a lower power on the pectorals, shoulders, arm, and back muscles.

CHAPTER 6…………COMMON TREADMILL Wounds CAUSES AND Extreme Manual for Keep away from THEM

It's generally so invigorating to have this new wellness plan. Maybe you haven't been watching your eating regimen throughout the previous few months, and presently you have cut a few pounds. Indeed, whichever the reason that sends you running on that treadmill presumably got you asking-How safe are these toys? What is the likelihood of winding up with a treadmill injury? Most likely not quite so protected as you naturally suspected. As per a post by Angela Haunt on the Washington Post 'How to guard yourself and your children around your home treadmill, north of 15,000 Americans have been treated for treadmill-related wounds over the recent years, with a couple losing their lives. Sounds very difficult. How then might you at any point securely happen with your arrangement on a treadmill? Furthermore, is it simpler to run on the treadmill in fact? Attempting to stroll before you slither It is critical to have a wellness plan or routine and wellness objectives. All things considered, the objectives will be good for nothing on the off chance that you end up with treadmill foot agony or lower leg torment, hip torment or crack, treadmill injury, or most dire outcome imaginable you lose your life essentially on the grounds that you needed to accomplish your objectives too early. Once in a while clients will generally become restless with themselves, invest an irrational measure of energy working out, push past their bodies "flexibility limits", and therefore get injured.

Getting off-daily schedule: Following a lot of time work or rest or simply rest, your body needs to have a little window to heat up only a bit of spot before the lively activities. This warm-up assists increment with blooding flow in the body, which helps an extraordinary arrangement in forestalling irritation. Getting off the bed and bouncing on the treadmill, for example, may prompt hip torments on the off chance that you didn't do some stretches first. Each wellness routine has warm-up works out; going "off-script" causes treadmill wounds. Broken down or unseemly work-out gear Running on a shoe with an exhausted heel messenger will cause lower leg torments, having tight or inelastic jeans can cause falls. Fundamentally, having unseemly or broken down gear causes wounds, and this isn't simply on treadmills. **General well being neglect:** Sprinters here and there will more often than not ignore some security rules while utilizing treadmills, for instance, different sprinters don't have the foggiest idea how to utilize treadmill well being key for crisis stops. Others watch their feet while running as opposed to looking forward, some step on moving treadmills. These, among different ignores, bring about minor and significant treadmill wounds.

Normal Treadmill Wounds, We will examine the normal wounds

and how utilizing the treadmill can achieve such wounds.
Hip Wounds: Late night of working out on the treadmill-either running or grade strolling, sharp torments can be capable on the hip bones while strolling, twisting, or hunching down. Hip torments are brought about by putting an excessive amount of weight on the hips. Torn or wounded tendons or ligaments or sore solid tissues can bring about hip wounds. This can be ascribed to utilizing strange step designs or overextending one's legs to an extreme.
Falls: Falls are one more typical treadmill injury and can be credited to many variables. Great many yearly treadmill wounds are from falls. An absence of focus can cause falls while running or strolling on the treadmills. One more typical reason for falls is an ill-advised utilization of the security key, and others fall by taking a gander at their feet as opposed to looking forward. Falling can prompt serious wounds like consumes from the warmed cushions, head injury, and lower leg or knee wounds.
Heart entanglements: Heart issues, for example, cardiovascular breakdown and respiratory failures can be auxiliary to other hidden ailments. At the point when people with related fundamental ailments figure out seriously on the treadmills for extended periods, they can have assaults related.
Shoulder wounds: Shoulder wounds come about because of utilizing handrails at high paces. In specific occurrences, shoulder disengagement was accounted for, while different clients experienced sharp torments following some serious time running or strolling on the treadmills. Most of these wounds can anyway be restored with a submerged treadmill, wounds, for example, knee torments, Achilles tendinitis among other treadmill wounds.

The most effective method to Stay away from Treadmill Wounds.

Get the right cog wheels This isn't nonessential. You can't run on broken down shoes, unyielding jeans and play it safe. For example, have the proper stuff, suggested shoes, for example, sprinter elastic shoes, shorts, and cots. Wear the proper stuff fittingly. It isn't sufficient to Have the right stuff. Wear the cog wheels suitably. For example, tie your shoes accurately, don't leave binds freely hanging, and have your garments well fitted. Try not to step or hop on a running treadmill. You will in all likelihood fall assuming you do this-the machine will presumably mislead you. Ensure that your treadmill is off prior to getting on. **Concentrate:** Abstain from utilizing your telephone or watching a mounted television. You ought to likewise try not to converse with individuals close to you and checking out at your feet while utilizing a treadmill. Essentially, keep away from disastrous exercises. Keep off the handrails if conceivable. While turning out for an uncommonly significant time-frame, you ought to keep away from the handrails however much as could be expected. Have sufficient room behind you. You would rather not hit yourself on a seat or a free weight when you incidentally slip. Abandon space you. Continuously get youngsters far from the treadmills. Keeping youngsters off the machine ought to be finished nonstop, whether the machine is on or off. Power off the treadmill. Continuously leave your machine fueled off after use.
Treadmills and Floors-A Mark of Concern.
Frequently, sprinters whined of machines destroying their floors over the long haul, particularly those with hardwood floors.

Machines and floors are a mark of concern. Utilizing mats can assist with shielding your floor from the ruin brought about by working the machine. While introducing the machine, it is in this manner essential to utilize a treadmill mat for hardwood floors to keep away from harm.

Do Treadmills Cause Knee Wounds, How Would You Forestall Knee Wounds.

Knee wounds are a portion of the normal treadmill wounds revealed throughout the long term. An article posted on the Treadmill Audits gave clarifications on discoveries of Philip Wealth, a specialist in bio-mechanics. He made sense of that running with no grade can bring about knee wounds. Running and strolling on the treadmill with no grade causes serious knee wounds or future confusions, muscles are stressed because of the upstanding stance, particularly during a delayed sudden spike in demand for the treadmill. Knees can't retain shock in this movement, and this, over the long haul, makes harm the knee. Sprinters have announced symptoms of treadmills on knees. Some of the time the simple running on the treadmill negatively affects the knees and results in difficulties as minor as tendon injuries to difficult issues like serious tears. Forestalling treadmill knee injury You should run in a somewhat slanted stance of around 3% is prescribed to stay away from unnatural strolling or slanted designs, run appropriately on the treadmill to keep away from wounds. It would be prudent assuming you safeguarded the jeopardized joints by setting the treadmill to a slope position to assist the knee with retaining shock from the activity. Begin by strolling gradually and slowly pace up. Firing up leisurely will help the joints slowly change in accordance with the rising pace. Utilize short walks rather than long walks. Short walks will overwhelm the tissues and muscles of and around the knee. Converse with your medical services supplier prior to getting onto a sprinter in the event that you have related previous circumstances.

Treadmills and Sore Lower legs: Without a doubt, treadmills cause sore lower legs. Lower leg irritation is a typical objection by numerous sprinters. Sore lower legs are credited to overspending. A few sprinters utilize high rates that are unnatural to them for significant stretches. This strange way of behaving can bring about lower leg irritation. The associating muscles between the shin and the lower leg some of the time cause irritation before the lower legs. Continuously stretch the calves hurt on the treadmill and use lower speed cutoff points to cure this. Another well known way that treadmills hurt lower legs is out of abuse. Sprinters will generally in a flash drive themselves to outrageous levels rather than continuously developing into them to accomplish; they will quite often abuse resolve gear like treadmills. Abusing gear make wounds a few pieces of the body, including the lower legs. The smooth running on treadmills empowers longer running, which some of the time becomes undesirable.

Pele ton Treadmills-Wounds and Passing. A post on the Lawful Inspector US made sense of that in May 2020, Pele ton reviewed all its sold treadmills after the passing of a six-year-old youngster. Moreover, the organization had detailed 72 wounds because of their machines. The wounds were very extreme broken bones, profound cuts, consumes, and wounds. The US Shopper Item Well being Commission gave a public caution and mentioned Pele ton to review their broken machines. The treadmills had engines that required higher ground freedom contrasted with different treadmills. Their touchscreen was additionally separable, and this made them less protected. An assertion delivered later by Melton recognized that they have worked on their items and that the specialized issues on the Pele ton machines were tended to. They, in any case, didn't specify that the fixes included machines sold external the US.

Is Running External a Superior Choice. Running external accompanies numerous wild factors, for example, weather patterns, time factors, ecological well being as a general rule, in addition to other things. Notwithstanding its dangers, I can reason that treadmills offer better circumstances. Treadmills make you quicker since it's simpler to screen your advancement and get to the next level. You can run whenever you feel, no matter what the climate or other ecological elements, gave you have power. Suppose on a frigid day, you can run more easily on a treadmill than outside. The dangers related with treadmills are controllable, and well being measures can be attempted to forestall treadmill wounds. Except if you are a competitor, who requires both indoor and outside running, treadmills are recommendable.

End: Treadmills offer an exceptionally helpful approach to participating in a running or strolling exercise, you can run in the solace of your home or rec center at some random time. You don't need to stress over the virus outside dialing you back or that tempest or snow preventing you from running. All things considered, that is only the cherry on top of the cake, with treadmills, you can screen your advancement in genuine speed and miles covered. Sounds energizing! However much we commend the accommodations, we genuinely must comprehend and lay out that there are takes a chance with engaged with utilizing treadmills. Continuously guarantee that you practice the well being measures and safe utilization of the hardware. Pick your number one treadmill, make a point to go securely about everything, and partake in your running or strolling.

Habitually Sought clarification on some pressing questions.
QUESTION 1.What is a well being key on a treadmill?
A security key is a key connected to one finish of the treadmill, for the most part the front board, and the opposite finish to the client. The key gives a quick crisis stop to the machine.

QUESTION 2.Which Pro Form treadmill is awesome?
Numerous clients, from surveys checked, favored the Pro Form CST-Shrewd. Different clients favor Pro Form Master 2000-Brilliant. This specific model accompanies a 10" HF touchscreen in addition to a 30-day i Fit family enrollment, finally the Pro Form City L Collapsing likewise bested the rundown. With its km/h speed regulator and 30-day i Fit family enrollment, sprinters adored it.

QUESTION 3. Which is the best Nordic Track treadmill to purchase?
Most of the business purchasers favor the Nordic Track Business 1750

QUESTION 4.Which is the best treadmill for home use?
Most of homegrown purchasers went for the Nordic Track 1750

QUESTION 5. Which brand of treadmill is awesome?
At the first spot on the list of client suggested treadmill brands was the Nordic Track with the 1750 model as the most liked. Running up was the Sole Treadmill, with the F-80 as the most liked.

CHAPTER 7.........ADVANTAGES Of Submerged Treadmill

Generally, sprinters had not many choices and little mindfulness in regards to actual wounds in their joints and muscles. They could either prepare through the injury or rest until they recuperate. Today, be that as it may, numerous assets can help you in your throb and agony. One such asset is a submerged treadmill, which numerous competitors favor while running is definitely not a prompt choice. Here's the reason!
As you probably are aware, your body may not perform well with full-weight-bearing movement while you're encountering muscle torment or recuperating from a physical issue. Fortunately, submerged treadmills permit clients to run at a lower level of their body, like preparation on a zero-gravity treadmill. Also, it builds the opposition and diminishes the running effect. Thus, regardless of whether you're in fact running submerged, the hardware guarantees you're actually getting a respectable exercise. Strangely, those are by all accounts not the only advantages of submerged treadmills. This article features the absolute most striking advantages of strolling in water.

How Does a Submerged Treadmill Function.
Most submerged treadmills consolidate land-based exercises with water's benefits the lightness standard and hydrostatic tensions. This permits the body to keep up with muscle memory for ordinary

exercises like running and strolling. Simultaneously, the preparation permits muscles to work better over the long haul for better portability, assisting patients with recapturing coordination. In addition, submerged treadmill treatment helps them support and work on their adaptability, step, and equilibrium.

What's Hydrostatic Strain: By definition, hydrostatic tension alludes to the strain/force brought about by the water encompassing the submerged body parts, making delicate opposition and backing. This outcomes in equivalent strain around the body, accordingly diminishing pressure and expanding on the joints and expanding adaptability. Moreover, running or strolling in water makes more prominent obstruction than playing out a similar movement ashore. Even better, it increments cardiovascular strength and muscle tone, particularly assuming you join submerged treadmill preparing with weight-bearing exercises ashore.

What's the Lightness Rule: The lightness standard alludes to how much water that dislodges an individual's weight. All in all, your body will feel around 25% lighter assuming that you're preparing in water. This weight decrease diminishes the effect on your muscles and joints while working. However, more critically, it will lessen the effect powers on existing wounds, permitting you to begin treatment sooner while holding your muscle molding and strength.

Advantages of Submerged Treadmill Running.

1. Works on cardiovascular endurance: The primary advantage of utilizing a water treadmill to run submerged is it creates more prominent cardiovascular perseverance. In particular, submerged treadmill exercise based recuperation includes longer exercise terms joined with expanded water obstruction. This assists with expanding your on-ground actual endurance. In this manner, submerged treadmills can be utilized as cardiovascular wellness gear for patients unfit to practice ashore after a medical procedure. Over the long haul, the preparation will reconstruct the patient's solidarity and eliminate joint pressure.

2. Muscle and joint unwinding: Submerged treadmill treatment assists with lessening muscle and joint torment, particularly in more established individuals. Additionally, strolling on a submerged treadmill can essentially lessen the aggravation or fix persistent circumstances like osteoarthritis. On account of the regular hydrostatic strain of water, which goes about as the wellspring of mending powers for the treadmill. Simultaneously, it diminishes enlarging, helps adaptability, further develops strength, and loosens up joints.

3. Advances walk preparing: Practicing on a submerged treadmill like the Hydroworx treadmill is one of the most incredible ways for step preparing for any individual who is finding it challenging to walk. One explanation is that a water treadmill permits patients to do stride preparing without the apprehension about falling. Also, it causes older patients to have a solid sense of safety, empowering them to go to submerged treadmill non-intrusive treatment meetings. As per measurements, around 30% of grown-ups over age 65 experience a fall yearly, primarily due to the debilitating of their bodies and absence of equilibrium. Accordingly, clinicians need to have hardware that assists patients with recovering their equilibrium. In such manner, numerous doctors suggest submerged treadmills as the ideal hardware for low-influence walk preparing. Plus, submerged treadmill preparing further develops walk designs by duplicating the biomechanics of land developments. Basically, these treadmills advance a more regular walk design than preparing in a static pool. This makes legitimate biomechanics in a low-influence climate and moves them to land developments.

4. Fortifies muscles: Muscle strength is one of the most neglected elements of the multitude of advantages of strolling in water. However, as per late Texas An and M College research, joining water treadmill activities and strength preparing fabricates weight more really than doing strength preparing alone or along with standard treadmill works out. At the point when you run on a water treadmill, your body encounters more prominent effort in view of the water's consistency. This outcomes in critical enhancements in center muscles all through your body and more noteworthy leg, foot, and hip strength.

5. Increments adaptability: The other extraordinary advantage of preparing on a water treadmill is expanding the patient's adaptability. As currently referenced, preparing submerged decreases an individual's load by up to 80%, diminishing weight on the joints. All the more remarkably, the tangible impacts of water permit patients to appreciate more muscle and joint unwinding. This outcomes in higher adaptability, particularly when joined with various cardiovascular exercises and developments one encounters on the treadmill for the pool.

6. Diminishes joint firmness: A new report directed by Utah State College laid out that submerged treadmill treatment lessens joint torment and increments versatility in patients with osteoarthritis. In another examination, the quantity of Americans experiencing osteoarthritis, which expanded from 21 million to 26.9 million from

1990 to 2005, will positively increment as time passes. Along these lines, a submerged treadmill will be a significant exercise based recuperation for patients with osteoarthritis.

7. Diminish circulatory strain levels: Like some other activity, preparing on a submerged treadmill diminishes hypertension. This makes it truly outstanding and best activities to do consistently. A new Texas An and M College research even proposed that submerged treadmill practices are more successful at diminishing pulse than land-based exercises. As per a review that dissected 60 grown-ups contrasting submerged and on-ground treadmill exercises, water treadmill preparing prompted a more noteworthy decrease in diastolic pulse. Hence, submerged treadmill preparing is an ideal exercise choice for north of 67 million patients experiencing hypertension in the USA. The majority of these people keep away from land-based exercises in view of agony.

8. Builds reinforcing and mending of harmed tissues: Likewise, preparing on a submerged treadmill advances the recuperating of harmed tissues. Simultaneously, the machine can be utilized for stride preparing to work on patients' actual versatility, lessen different circumstances like osteoporosis and further develop strength. Also, this preparing can be joined with stream treatment in active recuperation for patients with firm muscles to decrease torment and further develop portability.

9. Advances early scope of movement: Individuals experiencing persistent circumstances, for example, osteoarthritis normally keep away from exercises like actual activity and strolling. A similar case applies to more established grown-ups with muscle and joint torment. Curiously, submerged treadmill treatment can make a

portion of that aggravation vanish. Simultaneously, water has regular hydrostatic strain, which helps the mending system in patients with ongoing torment conditions. Plus, patients just bear around 20% of their bodies while they are chest-somewhere down in the water. Simultaneously, midsection profound water will decrease your body weight by around half. Whichever the case, this lessens the effect powers on existing wounds, permitting you to begin treatment sooner while holding muscle molding and strength. What's more, the preparation helps unwinding diminishes expanding, supports adaptability, loosens up joints, and further develops strength.
10. Weight reduction benefits: Finally, strolling or running submerged can assist individuals with weight issues shed off certain pounds. The solace and lightness presented by submerged treadmill conditions make the exercises seriously moving and pleasant for corpulent grown-ups. In 2009, research led by Texas An and M College included 57 stout grown-ups relegated 3 week after week exercise meetings on a submerged treadmill. The members kept up with their day to day exercises and diets over the 12-week study. The report of this study exhibited that the members showed significant upgrades in the weight record and hip-to-abdomen proportion contrasted with comparable land-based examinations. All the more critically, this exploration laid out that submerged treadmill preparing fundamentally works on high-impact limit and decreases muscle to fat ratio and weight, no matter what the eating routine. Also, the members experienced critical decreases in pressure related body torment in light of submerged treadmill treatment.

Normal Purposes of Submerged Treadmill Preparing. Athletic mentors and actual specialists regularly utilize submerged treadmills to assist patients with working on their solidarity or keep competitors in shape during a physical issue. A portion of these purposes are;

Forestall injury: As you probably are aware, all leg developments in the body are associated with the hips. Hence, any injury that influences the hip can bring on additional wounds around your body. To keep away from that, it's critical to perform hip-reinforcing exercise projects to decrease leg tendon (front cruciate tendon) tears yearly. Submerged treadmill exercises are viewed as one of the best methods for forestalling leg tendon wounds. Because of solidarity building benefits and alleviating variables to limit enlarging of preparing on a water treadmill. On the off chance that you've recently experienced a tear, submerged treadmill preparing can forestall further wounds and secondary effects like the deficiency of portability, muscle strength, and equilibrium.

Further develop stride after a physical issue. Recuperating from a leg or hip injury through step and recovery treadmill preparing can extensive and deter. Yet, all things considered, recuperation is a significant stage to continue your life as typical, paying little heed to how it takes. Submerged treadmill treatment meetings give remarkable advantages to patients that need to recapture their ability to stroll after joint a medical procedure. As a rule, submerged preparing permits you to walk sooner than ashore in light of the diminished weight-bearing water lightness. What's more, restoration treadmill preparing essentially decreases your possibilities falling, empowering you to remain committed and sure about your recuperation. Furthermore, water assists patients with amending broken stances they could have created post-injury and reinforce through obstruction. Increment leg muscle strength Preparing on a submerged treadmill has been demonstrated to tone leg muscles. As indicated by late examination, rotating ashore strength exercises with water treadmill preparing prompts more prominent lean weight upgrades than just doing ashore strength preparing. Additionally, ensure you eat quality food varieties consistently to expand the adequacy of your solidarity preparing.

End: By and large, submerged treadmills are utilized for patients with muscle or joint issues. Thus, on the off chance that you're experiencing actual injury and are not gaining any headway with your standard treatment, it's no time like the present you evaluate these astonishing advantages of submerged treadmill preparing. The main disadvantage with this hardware is that purchasing a home submerged treadmill for individual use is very expensive. On the other hand, you can go to a checked restoration place, facility, or wellbeing focus and train on the machine at a sensible cost.

Habitually Sought clarification on some pressing questions.
1.Question Are submerged treadmills great for your knees?
An intense exercise period on a submerged treadmill emphatically impacts joint pain related joint torment and joint precise speed. Hence, submerged treadmills are great for your knees as they can be utilized as a moderate treatment to ease osteoarthritis torment and further develop lower-limit joints' rakish speed.

2. Question For what reason is submerged treadmill preparing great for competitors? Submerged treadmill running permits competitors to connect with different muscle gatherings and give obstruction, working on their general strength and adaptability. Plus, submerged treadmill preparing expands their fit bulk more than obstruction preparing and land preparing.

3. Question Where might I at any point utilize a submerged treadmill?
These frameworks are ordinarily tracked down in non-intrusive treatment facilities and athletic preparation rooms. Notwithstanding, some versatile submerged treadmill producers sell units you can place into a current pool.

4. Question What sorts of submerged treadmills are accessible?
Submerged treadmills can be sorted into 2 kinds; Unsupported tub (mechanized submerged treadmill) and standard treadmill for pool/recovery tub. The first framework comprises of an unsupported tub with a mechanized belt, the capacity to turn on planes to increment obstruction, and movable water levels. Also, water on these tubs can be warmed to around 90 - 95 degrees to lessen weakness, advance adaptability and assist the muscles with unwinding. Unsupported submerged treadmills are made by organizations like Hydro Physio, HydroWorx, and Hudson Amphibian Frameworks.

Then again, recovery tubs include more insignificant treadmills set into a standard pool. A few models have customizable speed settings for the moving belt, while others are self-pushed. All the more critically, the water level in these frameworks ordinarily relies upon where you place the treadmill in the pool. These treadmills are made by organizations like Aquabilt, Hydro Physio, and Hudson Oceanic Frameworks.

5. Question What wounds can be utilized for restoration with a water treadmill?

A submerged treadmill can be utilized to deal with running wounds like nonexclusive knee torment, Achilles tendonitis, ITBS (Iliotibial Band Disorder), and plantar fasciitis. Likewise, the hardware can support restoring wounds, for example, breaks, upper leg tendon reproduction, lower leg hyper-extends, and other knee wounds. Note that submerged treadmill preparing doesn't fix wounds. All things considered, it offers a way to revamp muscle strength and keep up with wellness, hence accelerating the recuperation.

CHAPTER 8............TREADMILL In Loft Most Significant Interesting Points

Purchasing a home treadmill is an extraordinary other option if you would rather not go to the exercise center. Even better, it will permit you to consume calories and work-out consistently at home as opposed to going for an open air run. Sadly, this can likewise be a major issue, particularly on the off chance that you intend to involve the treadmill in high rises. One explanation is that treadmills are weighty hardware and can be exceptionally boisterous during use. Additionally, you really want to consider whether the floor of your loft will deal with the treadmill weight and different factors like space. Consequently, you need to devise imaginative ways of assisting you with practicing in a condo without upsetting neighbors or harming the floor surface. In this article, I'll take a gander at every one of the factors to assist you with concluding whether involving the treadmill in a loft is reasonable.

Could You at any point Involve a Treadmill in a Condo. Involving a treadmill in a condo offers different advantages since it permits you to practice in the solace of your home. Nonetheless, before you purchase a loft size treadmill, there are a few fundamental subtleties you really want to sort out. They include:

Rent arrangement: The principal thing you want to do before you carry a treadmill to your loft is to go through the rent understanding. This is on the grounds that some rent arrangements preclude treadmills. In certain cases, landowners don't consider treadmills while drafting lease arrangements. All things being equal, the agreement might allude to the treadmill in a roundabout way by naming it as a commotion understanding. On the off chance that you think the rent is muddled, look for affirmation from your renting office or landowner.

Condo size: Treadmills are accessible in different sizes. Thus, before you choose a particular model, check whether your loft has sufficient room to oblige it. Assuming the treadmill is enormous, you'll experience issues fitting it in your condo. Simultaneously, you've to consider how you will get it into the loft. Plus, most lifts have a weight limit that directs the greatest measure of burden they can deal with. You can undoubtedly pass this cutoff with a weighty treadmill and every one individuals expected to convey it. On the brilliant side, you can undoubtedly find a condo size treadmill with such countless sorts of treadmills accessible. These treadmill models are more modest than the bigger units expected for business use in the rec centers. Even better, most treadmills come unassembled, permitting them to effortlessly fit through the entryway. With everything taken into account, it means quite a bit to gauge the accessible space in your condo to decide the ideal treadmill size for you.

Electrical prerequisites: Like other home treadmill models, you really want to consider when you'll connect your treadmill in the condo. It's fundamental to approach the fitting electrical plug to work out with your machine. In such manner, most home treadmills are connected to standard 120v grounded committed electrical plugs. Besides, you might have to utilize a flood defender in the event that you don't plan to turn off your treadmill after each utilization. Then again, modern treadmill models normally consume greater power and require particular outlets. Moreover, such models can't be utilized in lofts since you can't change the power source. In this way, try not to purchase a treadmill that needs a unique outlet if you have any desire to take it to your loft.

Season of purpose: Running on a treadmill produces commotion, which can disturb your neighbors. For that, you've to consider the time you'll involve the treadmill in your condo. The commotion level will without a doubt be an issue in the event that you mean to involve the treadmill in the late night or early morning hours. Furthermore, you would rather not awaken your neighbors or keep them up since they're considerably more liable to whine to the property manager. All things considered, utilize the hardware during explicit times when others are working or not home. This will give you more opportunity in regards to commotion delivered while involving a treadmill in a condo. Additionally, tell your neighbors while you're intending to utilize the machine and see that timetable. Assuming that your treadmill is still clearly, I'll show different tips you can use to make it calmer or decrease the effect of its commotion on the environmental factors.

The most effective method to Decrease Treadmill Commotion in a Loft.

In the first place, it's fundamental to comprehend that treadmill commotion comes from 3 sources. That is, your feet while running/strolling, treadmill vibrations sent to the floor/wall, and the commotion of the treadmill belt/engine. Considering that, the accompanying tips will assist you with limiting the commotion produced by these sources.

Utilize a commotion diminishing activity mat for the loft. Putting a thick, elastic mat under your treadmill in the condo lessens the vibrations from the gym equipment and pad the means you take while running. Furthermore, the mat safeguards the ground surface and offers the gear a more drawn out life. Far and away superior, it keeps the treadmill set up, making it more steady by keeping it from moving around when put on dangerous surfaces like wooden floors and tiles.

Soundproof your condo. To keep up with harmony among you and the neighbors, you ought to consider soundproofing your loft to limit the commotion from the treadmill. You can achieve that by putting your treadmill on a covered region, hostile to vibration treadmill mats or plug segregation cushions. This will assist with limiting commotion transmission to nearby loft units. Likewise, guarantee that the machine doesn't come into contact with any wall. Besides, consider introducing a couple of wall boards in the room you're wanting to set up the treadmill. This will assist with diminishing sound vibrations from the treadmill, permitting you to partake in the medical advantages of treadmill preparing without upsetting your neighbors.

Search for a quiet treadmill for the loft. The least demanding method for decreasing commotion in a condo is to purchase a really economical treadmill. A few treadmills are furnished with calm engines, while others have clearly engines. This frequently shifts in view of the force of the motor and nature of the treadmill. Likewise, you need to consider the sort and thickness of the material used to house the engine since it decides how much clamor from the machine. These days, foldable treadmills can squeeze into little spaces like storage rooms. Even better, these conservative models are intended to run discreetly and even have wheels for simple transportation starting with one region then onto the next.

Wear the right running shoes: Wearing the right sets of running shoes diminishes the effect commotion of feet on the treadmill belt. If conceivable, search for shoes that have sound-retaining materials. For instance, shoes with shock-retaining gel assist with diminishing treadmill commotion and ingest the effect from your feet during the activity.

Supplant broken down course: Assuming that your treadmill produces squeaking commotions during use, look at for worn direction and rollers. The bearings are connected to the rollers, so you might require a brief period to get to them. Assuming you figure out that the bearing is broken or broken down, supplant it to diminish the squeaking and work on the general capability of your piece of hardware.

Grease up the treadmill belt consistently. As a feature of treadmill support, it's vital to routinely grease up the running belt. Legitimate treadmill oil decreases erosion in the machine's moving parts and brings down the commotion created by the motor during use. Nonetheless, to achieve that, you want to slacken the treadmill belt first and utilize a legitimate grease. Moreover, guarantee the treadmill is completely kept up with and its belts are fixed properly. On a similar note, check the drive engine to guarantee it's liberated from flotsam and jetsam and soil development.

Play out a calmer run or stroll at a grade. Most treadmill commotion comes from the effect of feet raising a ruckus around town belt while working out. Thus, to bring down the clamor, you ought to have a go at playing out a calm run. Simultaneously, you ought to consider the level you're lifting your feet from the treadmill to build the effectiveness of your calm running. On the other hand, you can have a go at strolling at a high or medium grade as opposed to running. This will assist with decreasing the effect commotion since your feet won't raise a ruckus around town that hard. However the activity will be all around as viable as running and assist with working on your general wellbeing and execution.

Set Up your treadmill in an essential area. Your treadmill will reliably deliver a few commotions, even in the wake of doing all that we've referenced previously. Hence, it's fundamental for put it decisively where it tends to make commotion without diverting the neighbors. For example, you ought to take care of the treadmill from inside walls and as distant from spaces like the review room and room.

Where Would it be advisable for me to Put My Treadmill. The best spot to place a treadmill in the loft is close to a corner. This will guarantee extraordinary help under your treadmill and keep the structure from skipping a lot of when you begin running or running. Running against the norm, try not to place the gear in that frame of mind of the room. This is on the grounds that the focal point of the floors will in general move a great deal contrasted with the edges, prompting superfluous vibrations and commotion. Additionally, try not to place the machine in that frame of mind since it will begin squeaking once you start to run or run. To forestall this vibration, guarantee the treadmill sits on a level surface. This will guarantee that its base sits on a uniform surface, keeping it from bobbing with each step you take.

Could You at any point Involve a Treadmill in an Upper Floor Loft.

If you live in a townhouse or loft, utilizing a treadmill on the upper floor is totally OK. Be that as it may, utilizing the treadmill higher up might be under an optimal choice. All the more critically, there are explicit ramifications you really want to consider before you set up your exercise space. You need to ask yourself inquiries like.

How much weight might a higher up floor at any point hold.

In the event that the high rise is basically strong, its floors can without much of a stretch hold the heaviness of a treadmill and anybody utilizing it. To put it plainly, the most extreme weight a higher up floor can have will rely upon the apartment complex's development. For the most part, an appropriately fabricated floor can uphold around 50 pounds for every square foot. Hence, a 100 sq. ft. room can hold 5000 pounds without taking a chance with underlying harm. Returning to the issue of involving wellness hardware in a loft, you need to think about the heaviness of a typical treadmill. Generally speaking, the heaviest home treadmills weigh around 350 lbs, however a few models arrive at up to 455 lbs. All things considered, on the off chance that a 300-lb individual purposes a 350-lb pound, that is a consolidated load of 650 lbs. Albeit that

might appear to be a great deal, an enough fabricated floor will easily uphold that load easily. Be that as it may, assuming you're actually worried about the treadmill weight, put your wellness hardware over a heap bearing wall. On the other hand, you can set up the treadmill straightforwardly on top of the floor joist for additional weight-bearing limit. The other choice is to search for a lightweight treadmill for lofts. Albeit most floors can uphold even the most monstrous treadmill, lighter models are viewed as the best gym equipment for a higher up condo since they're more straightforward to move into position.
Will the treadmill harm my floor.
Gym equipment, with its significant burden, vibrations, and moving parts, represents a potential gamble to your home floors. They can make long-lasting harm your covered or hard floor, particularly in the event that you set them in a stable situation without putting a story defender under. Thus, most treadmill producers encourage proprietors to put a mat under the treadmill to forestall expected harm to the deck. This is The way the Treadmill Can Harm Your Floor! In the first place, while utilizing the wellness gear, its parts and effect could dive into your floor surface and mark/scratch hard floors. Likewise, the machine might catch your rug deck or crash its strands. What's more, treadmill greases might spill out and collect under the gear over the long run, accordingly staining the deck. To shield your floor from the treadmill, put a durable, thick elastic mat under the hardware. The mat will balance out the machine and safeguard your floor surface. Likewise, lift up the treadmill totally from the floor surface while moving it starting with one spot then onto the next with the guide of someone else. Pushing the treadmill

across the floor might cause gouges or scratches on hard floors or obstacle the rug. Furthermore, assuming your treadmill has wheels on the base, ensure you lift it up from the floor until the transportation wheels contact the floor. **The mat will balance out the machine and safeguard your floor surface.**

Notwithstanding being little and smaller, condo size treadmills can in any case be weighty and cumbersome. Consequently, it's great to have an arrangement before you bring the treadmill into a loft. All things considered, the accompanying tips with you to get the treadmill into your loft effortlessly. **1. Pick a foldable treadmill:** Search for a treadmill that is not difficult to overlap down or dismantle to make it less cumbersome. Likewise, figure out how to get and appropriately crease the machine prior to hefting it around. **2. Check for transportation wheels:** Treadmills with wheels are more straightforward to deal with and move starting with one spot then onto the next. In the event that the treadmill doesn't have devices, consider utilizing elective devices like a furniture cart to move it to your loft. **3. Measure the steps:** Measure the door jamb as well as the width of the lift/steps of your high rise. This will assist you with picking a treadmill that will fit through your condo. **4. Search for help:** A treadmill ought to be moved by no less than 2 individuals, particularly in the event that steps are involved. All the more quite, guarantee the more grounded individual is positioned at the base since that is where most weight is taken care of. **5. Wrap corners:** Finally, wrap the sides of the treadmill with a cushioning material like covers, particularly on the off chance that they're sharp or metallic. This safeguards individuals conveying the treadmill into your loft from being harmed or harmed. **End:**Having a treadmill in a condo is an extraordinary method for guaranteeing that you train consistently at home to remain fit and sound. Sadly, you may constantly get clamor grumblings from the neighbors, restricting how frequently you utilize the hardware. To stay away from that, it's crucial for search for ways of assisting you with utilizing the machine without diverting the neighbors. Curiously, the tips in this article will tell you the best way to involve a treadmill in a loft without upsetting your neighbors. Basically, they'll tell you the best way to lessen treadmill clamor in a condo while keeping the floor from being harmed.

Habitually Sought clarification on some pressing questions.
1. Question What are the best treadmill choices for a condo?
On the off chance that your rent understanding restricts involving a treadmill in the loft since it might upset different occupants, search for calmer choices. These incorporate; rowers, versa climbers, ellipticals, exercise bikes, edges, and air walkers.

2. Question Is it protected to set up exercise gear on the second floor?
Indeed, It's protected to utilize a treadmill on the second floor of a condo or present day home, furnished it consents to the ongoing construction laws. Most second-level floors can uphold a huge weight limit, including the typical load of a treadmill and the individual running on it.

3. Question Could I at any point utilize a Peloton track in a loft? You, as a rule, can utilize a Peloton treadmill on the off chance that you live on the base floor. This is on the grounds that Peloton treadmills are generally heavier and more hard to haul around than exercise bikes. Also, they make essentially more commotion contrasted with lighter treadmill models.

4. Question How to get a treadmill higher up? Eliminate all articles and furniture that might impede you while you're moving the treadmill. Put a treadmill mat where you will set up your treadmill. Search for something like one individual to assist you with moving the machine. Lift the running belt and overlay it up towards the treadmill console until it gets into place. Marginally slant the treadmill towards the treadmill toward the floor. Lift it up from your end while your associate lifts the far edge. Take the machine up the steps, enjoying some time off when essential. While stopping to rest, ensure you either set the lower or upper piece of the treadmill safely on a stage and have one individual hold it consistent from the contrary side. Take the gear to the planned area and put it on top of the mat.

CHAPTER 9......................THE Most effective Method To Even out A Treadmill

Purchasing a treadmill to accomplish your wellness objectives can get all of you energized. Be that as it may, the mission is yet to be finished on the off chance that you don't have the foggiest idea how to even out a treadmill. As per Spine-wellbeing, you will consume a bigger number of calories on a treadmill than on trekking while acting in-home active work and activities. While setting up your treadmill to further develop your wellness levels, it's essential to guarantee its level by changing its evening out feet. Assuming you work out on an unlevel treadmill, you risk your body wellbeing through wounds and conceivable mileage of the belt in view of misalignment. To make up for the lopsidedness in the event that you don't have a level surface, the following are a couple of things you ought to really look at prior to beginning a treadmill exercise. Level the treadmill, Really taking a look at the belt arrangement, Changes in accordance with the running belt, Break in the treadmill.

Level your Treadmill: While setting up the treadmill, it's fundamental for cause it to sit equally on a superficial level floor. You can accomplish this by a general look from two headings. In the first place, actually look at across the belt (side-to-side equality) and along the belt (front-to-back uniformity). No matter what the level, you are utilizing, consistently guarantee that the treadmill changes are at nothing or the middle. In the event that you need to make changes, consistently change each foot in turn. On the off chance that you're not persuaded that your treadmill is level, you can control it up, however solely after adjusting it as per the model determinations on the client manual. Once more, power it off and make the vital changes. Place the level along your treadmills belt length and check in the event that the air pocket vial is focused. In the event that not, change the treadmill feet by contorting clockwise or counterclockwise until the air pocket rests at the middle. Each foot changes freely, and one can have a slight grade making it higher relying upon the surface. In the wake of making the essential changes and the air pocket rests at the middle, your treadmill is protected to utilize, and you can proceed with your exercise with an alternate scope of movement.

Actually looking at the Belt Arrangement: In the event that the belt isn't as expected adjusted, the treadmill will not work flawlessly true to form. Realigning the belt is a straightforward interaction, however in the event that you are uncertain, you can call your neighborhood expert to make the changes for you. Prior to beginning the realignment cycle, consistently work-out the essential treadmill alerts. POWER OFF the treadmill while working or changing the roller. In the event that you have long hair, tie it back and take off all free dress that represents a gamble of injury by coincidentally stalling out on the rollers. At the point when the treadmill is turned on, get objects and your fingers far from the rollers and belt. At the point when the treadmill is moving, it doesn't stop right away when an article is caught in the rollers and belts, and this can cause heaps of harm or wounds.

The most effective method to make appropriate checks.

1. Prior to realigning the running belt, guarantee that the treadmill isn't perched on a lopsided surface.
2. Power on the treadmill in the wake of interfacing the fitting to a devoted circuit and let it run at a consistent speed for 1-2 minutes.
3. Set the speed to 5 kph (3mph) and tune in for any commotion from the belt or rollers.
4. Assuming there are any abrading clamors, power off the treadmill promptly to forestall further harm.
5. Actually take a look at the back of your treadmill to check whether the belt is fixated on the running bed. Assuming there's any float away from the middle, it implies that you want to realign the belt.
6. A frayed belt in light of misalignment is seldom covered by most guarantees. Supplanting a belt can be exorbitant, so it's essential to promptly adapt.

Changing the Running Belt: Subsequent to putting the treadmill in its level position or on a hard core treadmill mat, make sure that the treadmill belt has legitimate pressure and runs on the focal point of the running bed. You ought to never endeavor to change the treadmill belt when somebody is remaining on it or when it's turned on.

1. Find the belt change bolt on your treadmill's back left and right sides.

2. Take the side running out focus and change in like manner utilizing a customizable wrench by turning the ¼ clockwise or counterclockwise.

3. Make ¼ clockwise to the bolt in the event that the belt is askew towards the right half of the treadmill. Turn ¼ counterclockwise in the event that you really want to change the left side.

4. Continuously change the running belt ¼ turn each opportunity to abstain from over-fixing, which might harm your treadmill.

5. Power on to check the arrangement on the deck surface and rehash this cycle assuming the running belt is as yet skewed.

6. On most treadmills, just change the LEFT side bolt (Decide your left by remaining on the back confronting machine). Never change the right side except if vital, as fixing different problems is for the most part utilized.

Breaking In Your Treadmill: There is no conclusive period when you will totally break into your new unit. While moving your treadmill, putting away it, or while on the way being transported, parts like pinion wheels, direction, and belts could move awkward. On the off chance that this occurs, your hardware could run with a few harshness and even make scraping commotions as you power it up interestingly. Nonetheless, contingent upon the commotion level, the gear ought to run as expected subsequent to involving it for a couple of days. On the off chance that it doesn't consider every one of the above cycles and make the changes required.

Treadmill Wellbeing.

1. Treadmills are expensive and furthermore weighty. While moving them, be cautious and request help if fundamental.

2. Continuously move your treadmill when in an upstanding position or collapsed. When collapsed, guarantee that the lock hook is affixed to stay away from wounds.

3. Continuously plug your treadmill into a grounded power source.

4. Never power on a treadmill with a harmed line or fitting, regardless of whether it works appropriately.

5. Never power a treadmill that seems harmed or has interacted with water.

End: Treadmill practices assist you with being better and think better. You will find many surveys on Nordictrack treadmills for what it's worth among the top running hardware on the lookout. The most recent treadmill innovation incorporates an iFit Live program that utilizations Google Guides to mirror the track of a virtual course, in actuality. Continuously perform normal support checks to keep away from harms from a skewed treadmill belt. At this point, you have a thought of how to even out a treadmill. Luckily, it's not difficult to make manual treadmill belt changes at home.

Habitually Sought clarification on some pressing questions.
1. How to even out a treadmill on a lopsided floor?
Putting the treadmill on a lopsided floor might make it harm rashly. To keep away from this, change the back feet of the treadmill utilizing a level. Ensure the air pocket rests at the focal point of the vial.

2. For what reason is my treadmill shaky?
The belt can stretch or agreement relying upon the stickiness and temperature of the unit. A free string and a belt running off the middle demonstrate that your treadmill is skewed, which could make it unstable. Prior to involving your treadmill interestingly, consistently check that the running belt is adjusted accurately and that there is no strain on the belt.

3. Should the treadmill be level?
Indeed. In the event that the treadmill isn't level, the running belt could float or slip towards the inclining side. It might cause weight on the belt prompting mileage.

4. How would you adjust a lopsided treadmill?
Align your treadmill as per its model's details. Change the back feet ¼ turn clockwise or anticlockwise to make up for the lopsidedness.

CHAPTER 10..................THE Most Effective Method to Prepare For The Signal Test On A Treadmill Scarcely any Straightforward Advances

A blare test is one of the most incredible activities for testing your wellness level. In particular, this multi-stage test estimates greatest oxygen take-up and cardiovascular well being. Max oxygen take-up (VO2 max) decides how much oxygen the body utilizes while working out at most extreme exertion. All the more critically, this test is utilized by the military, police, people on call, mentors, and mentors to decide one's actual wellness level. In any case, might you at any point play out a signal test on the treadmill? That is one of the numerous things we'll be checking in this aide out. Likewise, we'll take a gander at certain impediments and advantages of preparing for the blare test on the treadmill.

What's the Blare Test.
The bleep or signal test is otherwise called the 20m transport run, multi-stage wellness, or PACER test. It's a famous test that Luc Leger initially created. Besides, it's utilized across the world by schools, military organizations including the English Armed force,

and sports clubs to improve cardio well being and decide wellness levels. By definition, the blare test alludes to a constant gradual greatest running test that is led up and down a 20m course. The crucial suggestion of the test is that there is an expansion in blare test running rate consistently. Likewise, the members should attempt to run a specific number of in the middle between per-modified blares. In such manner, a blare test sound track that contains the signals is typically played to give the members a sound market they can keep in time with. The more seasoned bleep test from the 1980s utilized a 400m outside track to play out the 20m transport run. All the more prominently, the point was to run between two spots 20 m separated on the caution of a recorded signal for a particular time frame, normally 1 moment. The recurrence of the signals increments as this test keeps, driving the members to get the running speed. Curiously, the first signal test is as yet being utilized today. Be that as it may, different renditions like Moderate Vigorous Cardio Perseverance Run (PACER) are ordinarily utilized in schools and preparing offices. Furthermore, there are 2 kinds of PACER tests; 15m and 20m variations. Basically, the blare test 20 meters PACER covers an all out distance of around 4740 m and requires something like 21 minutes to finish. Confidingly, the 15m variation has practically a similar combined time yet covers a complete signal test distance of around 4725 m. Significance of the Blare Test As I previously referenced, the blare test assists with evaluating oxygen consuming wellness. It's usually utilized with experienced exercisers like competitors preparing for a contest. Playing out the test previously, during, and toward the beginning of the preparation will assist you with surveying the adequacy of your preparation program.

Simultaneously, it will assist you with deciding how much your cardio wellness has moved along. Moreover, this straightforward however strong test permits you to survey your maximal high-impact power (VO2 Max). VO2 Max shows how successfully your body conveys and uses oxygen to create energy while taking part in actual activity. As per the NSCA (Public Strength and Molding Affiliation), realizing your maximal vigorous power is critical since consuming more energy assists you with delivering more energy that guides in muscle constriction.

Might You at any point Play out a Blare Test on The Treadmill. Despite the fact that you can't imitate the signal test completely on the treadmill, you can prepare for one on the machine. This will further develop your wellness levels and increment your endurance. The treadmill can assist you with reproducing around the vast majority of the circumstances associated with a signal test, including the positive progress and running rate. Be that as it may, the consequence of rehearsing your blare test on a treadmill won't be straightforwardly tantamount to the consequences of the first test. For instance, you can't duplicate the quantity of turns and deceleration you'll perform during the test. Generally, the treadmill is an incredible piece of wellness testing gear for signal test preparing since it has a few advantages. In this way, we should begin from that point.

Advantages of Involving the Treadmill for Blare Test Preparing. Safe running surface: Treadmills are furnished with a safe moving belt to give a uniform running surface to actual activities. Accordingly, you can undoubtedly zero in on your running procedure without being worried about the place of the following pothole, as in outside running. Guarantees individual well being Treadmill running guarantees individual well being since it permits you to prepare in your home or at your #1 rec center. This makes it more secure than outside running, particularly on the off chance that you lean toward preparing around evening time or promptly toward the beginning of the day.

Permits you to control the speed: The capacity to control the speed while running assists with further developing your blare test score. Luckily, a treadmill gives you full control of your running pace. Like that, you can incorporate explicit exercises that address the various velocities engaged with a signal test.

Reasonable for unfortunate atmospheric conditions: Poor open air weather patterns are significant difficulties for exercisers who need to keep up with consistency in their gym routine schedules. Fortunately, a treadmill is an extraordinary choice in the event that you live in a district that has such circumstances. What's more, it will permit you to incorporate running into your signal test exercise no matter what the atmospheric conditions since it's performed inside.

Impediments of Signal Test Preparing on a Treadmill: While it's feasible to prepare for a signal test on the treadmill, this kind of preparing has a few restrictions you should know about. Potential security dangers The bleep test is maximal, importance you've to encounter an expanded responsibility until you feel drained and depleted. As such, the activity compels you to push your body until it can't stay aware of the pace of energy prerequisites. Playing out that kind of activity on the treadmill can be risky. For instance, treadmill running until the mark of weariness can make you fall over on the track belt, causing you a serious physical issue. To keep such issues from occurring, ensure you have somebody watching you while preparing. Likewise, connect a security rope among yourself and the machine to act as a well being anchor.

Absence of Sending force: While running outside, one truly pushes their body forward. Notwithstanding, this positive progress is practically missing while you're preparing on the treadmill. All things considered, the treadmill belt goes in reverse, so you're not moving. This adjusts the powers expected to run, subsequently influencing the result of your Blare Test. To fix this issue, add a slope to your treadmill exercise. This will assist with making up for the absence of sending energy, however it won't fix it totally. No replication for deceleration and turning Fundamentally, playing out a signal test outside expects you to shift your speed by decelerating to stop or advancing to meet the imprint. Likewise, the preparation includes taking sharp corners to run the alternate way. Sadly, these circumstances are hard to imitate entirely on the treadmill. To make up for the absence of turns on the treadmill, add additional time in your preparation. In addition, work on running on level surfaces with goes to address turning. This will assist you with creating molding and execution that will guarantee the progress of your Signal test. With everything taken into account, treadmill preparing is one of the most dependable reproductions of the Blare test conditions you'll get without finishing a genuine test recreation.

Instructions to Do the Blare Test on a Treadmill. The most ideal way to get ready for your bleep test is to perform it on an indoor rec center floor with lines or an outside/indoor track with a straightway. In any case, assuming you've no admittance to these offices, you can reproduce the preparation on the treadmill. Furthermore, treadmills are open since the vast majority have them at home nowadays. All things considered, here are the means you really want to follow to mimic a Blare test on the treadmill successfully.

Imitate the signal test speed and conditions. The best thing about treadmill preparing is that it permits you to pick the speed to reproduce different running circumstances. That adaptability makes it simple to duplicate the standard bleep test. Nonetheless, before you start, you really want to decide the best slope and running rate for the first level of this test. Luckily, generally suggested blare test norms make it simple to set everything up. To begin with, set the treadmill to a running pace of km/h and a grade level at1%. These settings emulate outside running and mimic similar degree of energy prerequisites. All the more significantly, these settings reenact the first period of this multi-stage wellness test that will cover a blare test distance of around 140m in 1 moment. Likewise, search for a signal test sound record that recreates the blares to make your preparation experience more reasonable.

Increment the speed at 1-min spans. After the first level, you really want to speed up at explicit stretches, generally 1 min. Curiously, a few treadmills can permit you to foster a pre-customized exercise plan. This will permit you to set up the speed spans in advance, making your exercise more straightforward to perform. In any case, in the event that your treadmill doesn't permit you to pre-program the settings, you can speed up physically. You ought to speed up by 0.5 km/h after each moment. This will duplicate the signal test's speed increment as the time between the blares diminishes. For instance, the greatest speed as a rule arrives at 18.5 km/h for the 20m bleep test.

Top Tips for Signal Test Preparing on the Treadmill. Incorporate a mix of long, slow running, and quicker blare test spans. To accomplish this, the American Chamber on Exercise recommends both LISS (low-force consistent state) and HIIT (Extreme cardio exercise) while practicing to increment vigorous limit. Try not to prepare the week prior to the blare test. All things being equal, train around a month and a half before the test to give you enough time for the necessary perseverance. Hydrate continually while preparing to keep your liquid steps up. Continuously stretch and warm up before the preparation, and cool down appropriately subsequent to working out. Begin gradually and increment the power and length of your exercise meetings, particularly in the event that you've not prepared much of the time before. Additionally, ensure you counsel your PCP prior to beginning the preparation. Play out a few reinforcing and conditioning exercises like crunches and press-ups towards the finish of your runs. Last Words Playing out a signal test on the treadmill is testing, however it's one of the best oxygen consuming tests for deciding your wellness level. Moreover, you don't for even a moment need the perceptible blares while preparing on a treadmill. Shockingly better, the machine comes furnished with buttons and a control center to assist you with knowing the particular speed you are running. What's more, a treadmill permits you to prepare in every weather pattern and whenever of the day. It upholds a few different speed exercises that you can attempt to build your VO2 max.

Habitually Sought clarification on some pressing questions.
1.question What amount of time does the blare test require?
The bleep test takes around 6 min and 51 sec to complete as the speed increments continuously at each level. As far as distance, you'll take care of around 1120m when you get to even out 7.5.

2. Question What does the blare test measure?
A signal test estimates VO2 Max (maximal oxygen take-up) and cardiovascular wellness.

3.question What is the best signal test application?
Networks is one of the most complete Signal Test applications. It permits clients to perform different signal tests and even plan their tests.
On the other hand, you can attempt Bleep Test Light, which is not difficult to utilize. Also, it shows ongoing signal test movement, maximal oxygen admission, current stage, and absolute distance covered while running.

4. Who holds the blare test world record?
Jose Romero is the Blare test's reality record holder, having finished a 17.1 signal test. He was a VFL/AFL player at Western Bulldogs (1995 - 2001) and North Melbourne (1988 - 1994).

CHAPTER 11……………. CAN I Plug My TREADMILL Into A Standard Outlet

Despite the fact that treadmills with strong engines need more current, they can keep going for a really long time assuming they are very much fueled. However, on the off chance that it encounters a straightforward influence issue, it can set you back truckload of cash. Besides, this wellness hardware consumes a ton of power, which can prompt perilous power floods. All things considered, in the event that you're wanting to purchase another treadmill, there are sure electrical prerequisites you really want to consider. Notwithstanding, in this article, we'll take a gander at whether the treadmill will breakdown in the event that you plug it into a normal power source. **Electrical Circuit Prerequisites for Treadmills** The power required for a particular treadmill shifts relying upon the model and maker. Be that as it may, most treadmill units run on 120V through a grounded or devoted electrical plug. Likewise, most treadmill makers suggest involving flood defenders that fulfill specific guidelines in the event of electric flow vacillations or power deficiencies. What's more, on the off chance that your electrical plug doesn't meet the electrical prerequisites of your treadmill, you're encouraged to search for an expert circuit tester. **Treadmill Voltage:** Symbol Wellbeing and Wellness make treadmill brands like Proform and NordicTrack work on a 120V circuit. Running against the norm, treadmills from different brands like Smooth Wellness need a 110V circuit. Curiously, treadmills from the two makers can be fueled by a similar outlet. Albeit a standard private outlet in the US is 120v, the genuine voltage goes from 117 to 124V. All the more critically, items evaluated for a 120-, 115-and 110V circuit are viable with a standard private 120 V outlet.

Could You at any point Fitting a Treadmill Into a Typical Outlet.

Most treadmill models can be connected to a normal outlet, gave it's on a 15 or 20-A circuit, contingent upon the wattage. Home treadmills need a 15A circuit, while business treadmill power necessities suggest a 20 A circuit. In view of that, fueling up your home treadmills while building a home exercise center will be an extremely thrilling undertaking. In the first place, notwithstanding, you should guarantee that you plan its power utilization as needs be on the off chance that you wish to utilize the machine securely for a very long time. The most ideal choice is to utilize a grounded, committed circuit at 120 V and 20 Amps. On the other hand, you can utilize a devoted circuit with 15 A, yet the gamble will be somewhat higher since 15A circuits utilize a lighter measure contrasted with their 20A partner. To be totally sure of forestalling electrical issues, treadmill producers recommend having a devoted 20A circuit at every possible opportunity. A committed circuit implies that no other gadget is associated with that circuit. This permits the treadmill to securely draw all the power it necessities to work. Furthermore, on the off chance that the circuit is shared, the treadmill may not get adequate power, prompting a more limited life expectancy and horrible showing.

Why Utilize a 20A Committed Circuit for Treadmills. In spite of the fact that treadmills can run on a 15A circuit, most treadmills need a different/devoted 20A circuit. Tragically, 15A circuits comprise of light wires, in this way expanding their possibilities causing power issues whenever imparted to other electrical gadgets. On the splendid side, you can keep away from this by getting a committed 20A circuit for your treadmill.

For what reason does the treadmill require a devoted circuit. Most treadmills that anyone could hope to find in the market are mechanized, and the engine needs up to 20A of accessible power. In this manner, utilizing a 20A devoted circuit kills the gamble of over-burdening the current 15A wiring, which can overheat with the eventual result of causing a fire mishap. Additionally, this wipes out the gamble of wearing out the treadmill engine in view of coming up short on the necessary power, accordingly voiding your guarantee. All the more quite, an essential house wiring design includes a common 15A circuit, so it takes care of different outlets. Furthermore, the circuit includes a 15A breaker to safeguard it in the event that numerous gadgets are connected to these outlets. This will make the electrical switch trip while associating the treadmill to such outlets. In any case, that won't occur assuming you utilize a committed 20A circuit.

WHAT Sort OF OUTLET DO A TREADMILL NEEDS.
A grounded outlet: The fundamental advantage of utilizing a grounded outlet is that it keeps treadmill clients from being stunned in the event of a short out. In particular, this outlet associates with the climate, giving a way of protection from the electric flow. Subsequently, they have a third spike that ought not be dismantled as it might influence your wellbeing and security. To guarantee you have an appropriately grounded attachment, contact a circuit tester to introduce it.
Grounded, the committed circuit at 120v and 20A
As referenced before, this is the choice for controlling your treadmill as it assists it with running for a more broadened period. Additionally, ensure you plug the treadmill into the closest electrical plug that provisions capacity to other home devices.
Flood silencer for treadmill: Stopping the power line of your treadmill straightforwardly into a devoted 20A outlet opens it to electrical floods. Thus, it's essential to turn off the machine when not being used to shield it from harm because of these floods. Be that as it may, to be worried about turning off the gear after each utilization, search for a devoted flood defender. The flood defender plugs straightforwardly into the electrical plug without requiring an additional line. The best part is that it safeguards your machine assuming that there is an unexpected power change in your home.
Treadmill Flood Silencer Necessities
As per treadmill makers, you ought to utilize a solitary outlet flood defender with a rating of UL 1449 TVSS (Transient Voltage Flood Silencer). Also, the silencer ought to have an electrical rating of 15A

and 120V, and UL stifled voltage rating of under 400V. All the more significantly, you ought to plug the silencer into a grounded out, then, at that point, plug your treadmill into the silencer.

TYPES LF Electrical plugs YOUR Ought to Keep away from COR TREADMILL.

Ordinary outlets with deficient power, similar to those with under 110V, can prompt a specialized error in the activity of the treadmill belt. Such issues can likewise occur assuming that you're connecting your treadmill to any of the accompanying kinds of electrical plugs. **Shared outlets:** Electrical machines are frequently associated with a similar circuit utilizing shared outlets and lighting controls. This restricts the circuit voltage, which might possibly harm gear that needs more power, similar to treadmills. In this way, try not to control your treadmill with a common outlet. **GFCI outlet:** Treadmills don't work with Ground Shortcoming Circuit Interrupter (GFCI) outlets since they're helpless against power vacillations. All things being equal, treadmills ought to be fueled by an outlet that guarantees a consistent circuit stream to safeguard them from blackouts and current vacillations. Utilizing a treadmill on a GFCI outlet will much of the time trip the breaker. **Flood defenders:** Most treadmill units are furnished with inbuilt flood defenders. Assuming that is the situation, interface your treadmill straightforwardly to the wall power source without a flood defender. End On the off chance that you're pondering purchasing or purchasing a treadmill, it's essential to consider where you'll put it and its power necessities. In such manner, you ought to remember that a treadmill requires an adequate power supply to successfully work. Most treadmills intended for home use can be connected to a normal outlet since their engines needn't bother with a great deal of force. In any case, I'd firmly suggest that you utilize an appropriately grounded and devoted 120-volt, 20-Amp circuit for your treadmill, particularly on the off chance that its engine produces 3HP or more.

Habitually Sought clarification on some pressing questions.
1.Question What number of watts does the treadmill utilize?
Treadmill wattage normally fluctuates relying upon the highlights and model of the machines. All things considered, a treadmill can use around 200 to 500 watts.

2.Question What size breaker for the treadmill would it be a good idea for me to utilize?
The power necessities of most treadmills utilize a 20A devoted circuit with a disconnected ground/impartial. This implies that each electrical plug you plug the machine into shouldn't have some other gadgets running on that circuit.

3.Question My treadmill continues to trip the breaker; what could be the reason?
Different reasons can make your treadmill trip the electrical switch. In the first place, in the event that the hardware is drawing an excessive amount of force, the breaker will outing to keep the circuit from over-burdening or overheating. Likewise, in the event that you associate the treadmill to an AFCI or GFCI outlet, the breaker will trip.

4.Question Could you at any point plug a treadmill into a 15A circuit?

On the off chance that the treadmill maker suggests it, you can interface your machine to a 15A circuit. Plus, most circuits work at a limit of 80% limit, so your treadmill will deal with under 15A more often than not.

CHAPTER 12..................STEP By Step Instructions To KEEP YOURSELF AND YOUR Children SAFE AROUND A HOME TREADMILL

Albeit a treadmill seems like easy to use wellness gear, it tends to be risky whenever utilized inappropriately. Truth be told, it's viewed as more risky than some other kind of cardio hardware, including paddling machines and elliptical. This is as per treadmill well being measurements, explicitly, the US crisis division treated 22,500 and 15,800 treadmill-related wounds in 2021 and 2022, separately. All the more significantly, around 20% of these wounds happen in youngsters, as the Cross country Kids' Emergency clinic Exploration Establishment proposed. Hence, on the off chance that you have this wellness gear at home, it's critical to notice well being insurances to keep away from treadmill risks for youngsters. This article contains different treadmill dangers that will assist with protecting yourself and your children from this exercise machine.

A Short History of Treadmill Wounds. The treadmill youngsters' well being issue turned into a main pressing issue when a 4-year young lady passed on in a grievous home treadmill mishap. From that point forward, different well being associations and media sources have announced a few instances of treadmill-related wounds. As per an Exploration, most treadmill wounds that happen to grown-ups north of 25 are brought about by strains or injuries. Notwithstanding, different wounds like cuts and consumes can happen, especially to kids. The U.S CPS laid out that in excess of 25,400 treadmill falls and wounds occurred in 2015. What's more, the bonus revealed around 30 passing between 2004 and 2013 were connected with treadmill wounds. On a similar note, the office claims 17 treadmill-related passing from 2019 to 2022. Continuing on, treadmill mishap insights for the years 2016 and 2017 shows that treadmill wounds are very normal among kids. For example, of the 570 wellness hardware related wounds for youngsters under 13 years in 2015, 134 mishaps were brought about by treadmills. Concerning kid security, the US Purchaser Item Well being Commission got more than 80 reports of grown-ups, pets, and youngsters being pulled under the treadmill. Surprisingly more dreadful, a 7-year-old kicked the bucket from a Peloponnese treadmill mishap, prompting a far reaching review of the Peloponnese Tread+ and Track treadmills in 2020. Likewise, the Customer Security Item commission gave an admonition of the treadmill's risks and an upsetting video of a 3-year-old getting found out under the Peloponnese Tread+ treadmill.

Why Treadmills Are So Perilous for Youngsters. Like most large equipment and modern transport frameworks, treadmills are not planned considering kids. Subsequently, they're almost certain to make wounds little children and versatile babies slithering or moving onto a moving treadmill belt to arrive at a more established kin or parent. For example, The treadmill belt can discard youngsters from the machine, prompting blackouts or bigger cracks. Simultaneously, the parent might be harmed and lose balance as the youngster goes after them. Likewise, little fingers, hair, and hands can get found out in the moving belt component. This can prompt issues like evacuation of muscles and skin, removals, breaks, serious consumes, and so forth. On account of Peloponnese treadmills review, the machines were viewed as more hazardous to kids. This is on the grounds that their running belt has individual unbending rubber treated tracks/braces rather than a ceaseless belt. Additionally, the gear sits higher off the ground, expanding the gamble of children being pulled under.

Treadmill Parts That Are Not So Youngster Cordial. The CPS gauges that 9,700 children more youthful than 6 years and 18,500 children somewhere in the range of 4 and 15 are impacted by treadmill wounds yearly. All the more quite, 20% of these wounds brought about removals or breaks. Treadmill parts answerable for these wounds incorporate.

Power lines: A few treadmills are outfitted with control center and power lines that are inside kids' range. Sadly, these lines represent a huge gamble to kids, as seen on account of the 4-years young lady passed on in a grievous home treadmill mishap.. In particular, children can choke themselves while playing with these strings. All things considered, consistently ensure you mount your treadmill ropes so that children can't contact them. On the other hand, you can utilize a wall power source that is unavailable to children or use connections to get the ropes so that children can't slip them around their necks. Far better, turn off your treadmill after an exercise and store the line away from your kids.

Hole: Treadmill transports highlight a moving belt that is typically associated with a metal bed. Besides, the bed is controlled by an engine and circled around 2 rollers (pulleys). This transport line might attract objects and under the running space while moving. Additionally, this makes it very hard to pull out captured body parts. To be exact, the treadmill moving belt can be especially risky to children's hands. This is on the grounds that most home treadmills include an enormous space between the belt and the deck that can trap little fingers.

Running track: By and large, youngsters start a treadmill, speed up and take out of control. This is on the grounds that they can't stay aware of the great treadmill speeds, making them outing and tumble off the machine. Additionally, a few children will generally embed their fingers around the running belt edges or between the moving pieces of the gear. This can prompt serious wounds like removal, slashes, or breaks.

Critical Security Cautioning for Treadmills and Kids. As the interest for treadmills keeps on expanding, it's vital to safeguard your children, pets, and yourself from the different risks related with the machine. Strangely, a couple of fundamental rules can assist you with accomplishing that. They incorporate.

Look forward while strolling or running on the machine. The most secure method for running or stroll on a treadmill is to keep your head up and look forward during the activity. Sadly, most learners, particularly the people who are new to treadmills, peer down at their feet or consistently check the treadmill console while running. This can occupy you from the run, making you lose equilibrium and tumble off the moving belt, prompting treadmill wounds. Besides, peering down while preparing on a treadmill influences your structure, causing back and neck torment. Peering down while running on a treadmill can likewise make you feel tipsy, particularly in the event that you've utilized the machine a couple of times. Likewise, venturing off the treadmill can likewise cause you to feel perplexed. Assuming that is the situation, clutch a fixed item until the nakedness dies down. All the more critically, consistently ensure you warm up and chill off when working out to stay away from such issues.

Keep away from interruptions. Performing different errands like noting calls, understanding messages, and messaging simultaneously while preparing on a treadmill is another variable that can prompt treadmill mishaps. Studies have even settled that messaging is the primary driver of wounds while strolling or running since it influences solidness and equilibrium by up to 45%.

Try not to step off a moving treadmill. A moving treadmill represents a threat to the client and anybody nearby. Consequently, it's generally critical to guarantee that the treadmill is totally stopped before you step off. Likewise, check the area of the crisis shut-off button prior to utilizing the machine. This will assist you with halting the machine rapidly in the event that you become harmed or a garment is stuck between the deck and treadmill belt.

Try not to push your body excessively hard. Pushing your body excessively hard while practicing on a treadmill builds your gamble of injury. Fortunately, most present day are outfitted with highlights that permit you to follow your pulse and other body capabilities. For example, you shouldn't surpass 80% of your objective pulse while preparing. Nonetheless, the body consumes calories productively while working at 50 - 70% of your objective pulse. Then again, surpassing 90% of your objective pulse can prompt serious medical problems like stroke and coronary episode.

Use Treadmill Well being Highlights. Most current treadmills accompany different inbuilt well being highlights, for example, the crisis stop framework. The framework generally involves a treadmill security, a signal for an emergency response, or both. Before you get onto your treadmill, painstakingly read the guidelines manual to figure out how to utilize the well being highlights intended for that particular model. The security key is a gadget that connects to one finish of the treadmill console and the opposite finish to the treadmill client. Like that, the gadget will make the treadmill stop quickly when you tumble to forestall further expected injury. In this way, when you're not utilizing your treadmills, keeping the security key away from the gear is really smart, particularly if you've small children around it.

Try not to clutch the handrails while preparing. Clutching the handrails for a significant stretch while preparing on a treadmill can overburden your shoulders and elbows. Likewise, it shows that the grade or speed is set excessively high and should be acclimated to an agreeable level. Not to fail to remember that it can make you inclined to foot and leg wounds or even cause you to lose your equilibrium. Simultaneously, harassing onto the handrails lessens the quantity of consumed calories since your center muscles are not designated as they ought to be. Going against the norm, moving your arms unreservedly is a more regular development, consequently decreasing the gamble of injury.

Leave sufficient room for the treadmill. Assuming you're wanting to place the treadmill in your home rec center, consider where you'll keep it. In such manner, don't put it close to a work area or a glass entryway to try not to get harmed on the off chance that you tumble off the treadmill belt. Thus, guarantee a lot of room between the machine and encompassing walls. Albeit different have shifting leeway necessities MAST Global suggests leaving around 1.5 feet on the two sides and 6.5 ft of free space at the rear of your treadmill.

Get youngsters far from the treadmill. Treadmills can be exceptionally risky for youngsters, particularly when appropriate security safety measures are neglected. Research shows that 2 - 5-year-old support more treadmill wounds than other age gatherings. While the Buyer Item Security Commission guarantees that in excess of 9,700 gym equipment wounds are archived yearly. Considering that, it's dependably really smart to eliminate the security key and store your treadmill away from youngsters when it's not being utilized. Likewise, as a parent, ensure your children are being regulated by one more grown-up while you're preparing on a treadmill.

How Would I Protect My Youngster on a Treadmill? Never leave running gym equipment unattended. Likewise, put an entryway up or lock the room where you store your treadmill to limit your children's admittance to the machine. Try not to let kids on a moving treadmill since they can without much of a stretch fall and get consume wounds or blackouts. Keep the treadmill ropes in a space small children can't admittance to stay away from any gamble of strangulation or gagging on them. Continuously keep the hardware pointing toward the room entrance. Like that, you will handily check whether any children leave or go into the room. Continuously utilize the well being key while preparing on a treadmill. All the more significantly, store that key in safe region kids can't reach when you're finished with your exercise. On the other hand, you can set a security code on the treadmill to keep kids from beginning the hardware freely.

Other Significant Treadmill Youngster Well being Rules: Make your treadmill inoperable when you're not utilizing it. Kids ordinarily run on treadmills to mimic their folks and more seasoned grown-ups. Sadly, they're not full adequately grown and tall enough to securely work the machine. Thu sly, it's essential to lock the treadmill away from their utilization. For example, you can lock or turn off the treadmill, keeping kids from turning it on. What's more, on the off chance that your treadmill requires a string or well being key to begin, keep it in a spot kids can't reach.

Make the machine more secure to utilize. Leave sufficient freedom space behind the treadmill to safeguard you in the event that you tumble off the back. Shockingly better, put a slight, sturdy piece of the mat for the treadmill on the floor covering behind, around, and under the machine to pad any falls. What's more, in the event that you have a collapsing treadmill, overlay it up after use and store it safely.

Regulate kids during treadmill use. Kids who use treadmills might fall and get lost the side or back of the treadmill. This can prompt head wounds, broken bones, and other youngster treadmill risks. That is the reason it's significant children are continuously being regulated by a grown-up while utilizing any gym equipment. Like that, you can quickly answer and give them a medical aid treadmill assuming any of these mishaps happen. Nonetheless, on the off chance that the youngster has supported a serious injury like a wrecked bone or head injury, look for clinical consideration right away!

Show more seasoned kids how to securely utilize the gear. On the off chance that your child is sufficiently developed to utilize a treadmill, gradually walk them through its security includes and working controls. Furthermore, tell them the best way to turn on the treadmill without a key and how to switch it off rapidly in the event that any issue emerges.

Purchase a Youngster's treadmill Finally, there are different manual treadmills plans for youngsters you can purchase for your more youthful kids. This gear sticks to children's treadmill well being principles and doesn't offer similar dangers as mechanized treadmills for grown-ups. A genuine illustration of such treadmills is the Redmod's Tomfoolery and wellness Children treadmill. This manual treadmill accompanies a non-mechanized belt and a no-tip plan. The best part is that it's great for youngsters matured somewhere in the range of 4 and 8 years.

End: Main concern, as you set up your home rec center, it is essential to guarantee that the space is childproof. All the more significantly, keep gym equipment like treadmills out of the range of pets and youngsters. Even better, this will assist with protecting yourself and your children while practicing at home.

Habitually Sought clarification on some pressing questions. Question-1. Could a 10-year-old utilize a treadmill?
Treadmill age limitations and rules on how old a youngster ought to be to utilize a treadmill are normally given in the client manual. Much of the time, the suitable age is over 13 - 14 years.

Question-2. Might you at any point put the treadmill close to the wall?
Never put your treadmill against a fixed item or wall. This is on the grounds that you can without much of a stretch get caught on the moving track belt assuming you fall, particularly in the event that you don't have satisfactory room behind the machine. Thu sly, the best spot to keep a treadmill at home is to make a whole exercise room.

Question-3. What number of children get injured on treadmills?
As per measurements, north of 3,000 children younger than 8 have encountered serious treadmill wounds throughout the last year.

Question-4. What are the normal treadmill gambles for youngsters?
Rubbing consume is viewed as the most widely recognized treadmill

risk for youngsters. What's more, kids playing close or on the treadmills might possibly experience serious consumes, minor consumes, or even lose their hands/fingers.

CHAPTER 13…………….. STEP by step Instructions To Gather Maxkare Treadmill

MaxKare treadmill is a respectable wellness gear brand that sells different hardware for homegrown use. Likewise, their machines include a savvy treadmill configuration, yet they include a bigger number of highlights than other hardware inside their cost range. Along these lines, on the off chance that you're searching for a reasonable treadmill for home use, Maxkare is your go-to mark. One more fascinating element about MaxKare treadmills is that they have an easy to understand plan. Subsequently, their treadmill models are somewhat simple to utilize and gather. In this aide, I'll tell you the best way to set up and gather the MaxKare treadmill bit by bit! Thus, how about we get directly into it.

MaxKare Treadmill Gathering Guidelines. As currently referenced, the MaxKare treadmill is generally simple to collect since the vast majority of its parts are gathered. In this way, you just have to associate its endlessly console pole to the fundamental center unit, which will take you under 60 minutes. The best part is that the hardware accompanies a directions manual to direct you through the interaction and every one of the devices you really want for MaxKare treadmill gathering. One more advantage of this lightweight treadmill unit is that one individual can gather it.

Furthermore, the MaxKare 2.5HP treadmill just weighs around 41.2 kg/91 lbs, so it's not excessively weighty. In any case, it's great to have someone else nearby to help you out for security reasons. Furthermore, putting the machine on a defensive elastic mat might be smart since it forestalls wobbling during an exercise. Also, it's essential to gauge the machine prior to getting it to decide whether you have adequate space in your home. Luckily, MaxKare electric treadmill has a foldable, space-saving plan that permits you to overlap it up after an exercise. As far as aspects, the treadmill measures 53.3" long X 26.18" wide X 45.9" tall. Subsequently, the ideal exercise region for this gear ought to be around 4' 4" long X 2' 2" wide and a roof level of around 7'. Simultaneously, this wellness gear might require a freedom of around 1 to 2 ft at the back and on each side for wellbeing reasons, particularly on the off chance that you'll involve it in a restricted space. With everything taken into account, clients with levels of between 4' 6" and 6' 2" can undoubtedly utilize this exercise machine. Something else worth focusing on about the MaxKare treadmill is that it's not difficult to overlay and unfurl, on account of the delicate drop framework and collapsing component. The machine measures 28.46" long X 26.18" wide X 46.4" tall when collapsed. All in all, its full collected length is diminished to close to a portion of its size when you crease it up. The delicate drop framework permits the running deck to self-lock while lifting it. Running against the norm, contact the kick button when you wish to bring down the deck, and the deck will delicately bring down itself utilizing the power through pressure. **Instructions to Collect MaxKare Treadmill Bit by bit.**

Stage 1: Read the guidelines: You really want to give close consideration to a few regions while gathering a MaxKare treadmill. To begin with, it's essential to guarantee that all parts are fixed immovably and adhere to the gathering directions accurately. On the off chance that the edge parts aren't fixed as expected, they'll appear to be free, causing the treadmill to produce bothering clamors during use. Likewise, there ought to be no development in the control center poles, gathering, or handlebars. Any play here shows that the machine hasn't been gathered as expected, which might wind up harming your treadmill. To stay away from such issues, survey the gathering guidelines and make restorative moves.

Stage 2: Pick the area of the treadmill: Before you unload your MaxKare foldable treadmill with an auto slant, pick the ideal area to put it. In a perfect world, the machine ought to be placed on a level surface. Also, there ought to be a leeway of around 6ft behind the machine, 3 ft on the two sides, and 1 ft in front for the power line and collapsing. On a similar note, guarantee the machine doesn't hinder air openings/vents.

Stage 3: Unloading: Put the treadmill container on a level surface while dealing with it with care. All the more prominently, put a defensive mat on the floor and never open the treadmill box when it's its ally.

In the wake of putting the container on the floor:

1. Eliminate the banding lashes.

2. Whenever you've done that, don't move or lift the unit except if you've collected it completely.

3. Guarantee you move it upstanding, collapsed position while keeping the wellbeing lock secure. Also, don't snatch the grade casing or attempt to move or lift the treadmill before it's completely collected. Ultimately, handle the unloaded machine with care to keep the high-pressure shocks from springing open, prompting injury.

Stage 4: Really take a look at the included instruments and parts: As referenced before, the MaxKare collapsing treadmill has every one of the devices you want to gather it. For instance, the machine accompanies a 6mm T-wrench and a 5mm Allen Wrench. Different parts that accompany this unit incorporate; 2 roller end covers, 3 equipment sacks, a control center get together, a security key, a silicone oil bottle, and a water bottle pocket. Like different treadmills, your MaxKare treadmill won't begin except if you set the security key ready. The key is intended to cut the treadmill power in the event of a fall. Thus, ensure you join the treadmill wellbeing key clasp end to your attire and check assuming it's functional like clockwork. Besides, you should guarantee that all fasteners and nuts are to some degree strung and set up during every gathering stage prior to fixing them totally. All the more critically, you can delicately apply some treadmill grease shower to make the establishment simpler.

Stage 5: Introduce the control center poles: Open the main equipment sack and slide the right control center pole on its help cylinder and utilize the bolts, spring washers, and curve washers on the facade of the control center pole to fix it. Do likewise for the two sides of the control center pole. Open the subsequent equipment sack and interface the control center to the upstanding pole on the two sides utilizing the included bolts, spring washers, and curve washers. Then, associate the control center links and circumspectly wrap wires up the control center pole to try not to squeeze or harming them. Simultaneously, ensure the control center link closes are firmly situated on one another and the prongs are adjusted. Gradually slide the water bottle holder into the opening in the treadmill console until they snap together. Ultimately, open the third equipment pack and crease up the treadmill, guaranteeing that the lock hook is safely locked in. Join the right roller end cap with the included bolts and do likewise on the opposite side.

Instructions to Crease up MaxKare Treadmill. To crease up your MaxKare treadmill, hold the back end and cautiously lift the finish of the deck into an upstanding situation until the security lock hook is locked in. Try not to allow the machine to go before the treadmill deck is safely locked. To unfurl the treadmill, solidly hold the back end and tenderly delivery the lock hook until it separates. Presently, cautiously bring down the treadmill deck to the ground. This foldable plan makes MaxKare quite possibly of the most effortlessly put away treadmill available. Stunningly better, it's furnished with advantageous transportation wheels incorporated into the edge. Notwithstanding, prior to moving it around, you want to guarantee that it's collapsed and locked. From that point onward, immovably hold its handlebars, slant it back and roll.

Instructions to Set Up a MaxKare Treadmill. Since this hardware accompanies a you'll find it very simple to keep up with, use and set up. In any case, it requires a smidgen more direction to guarantee legitimate use and gathering. All the more significantly, figuring out how to set up the MaxKare treadmill securely and accurately will assist you with getting the most ideal activity.

In light of that, here are the means you ought to follow while setting up your treadmill;

1. Gather the treadmill deck and control center: Much of the time, the bigger treadmill parts like control center, deck, and arms come preassembled. Accordingly, you just have to interface these components, and you're all set. Nonetheless, before you do that, pick an area for your machine and put the deck on the floor. As referenced, leave around 5 - 6 ft of free space behind the treadmill deck. This security insurance assists with diminishing injury assuming that you fall or excursion off the running belt. Then, associate the arms to the deck and solidly screw them. Presently, collect and associate the treadmill control center and continue on toward the following stage.

2. Associate the control center: Associate the control center to the treadmill to make the gear ready. The MaxKare treadmill has 2 or 3 wires that associate the link for speed and grade. Fortunately, these wires are named, so you just have to embed them into the assigned space. Nonetheless, guarantee you hide the wires to abstain from squeezing them while screwing the treadmill console into the arms.

3. Test running belt strain: Since the running belt of the MaxKare treadmill is normally pre-introduced at the assembling office, it may not require a lot of change. In any case, testing its strain prior to utilizing the machine is as yet significant. The running belt ought to lift no less than 3" from the deck assuming that it's appropriately tensioned. In the event that the belt is too close, the gamble for breakages or tears is high, which isn't great. What's more, you ought to guarantee that the running belt is appropriately tensioned in the deck since it could have moved during transportation. To realign the belt, fix the bolt on the deck until the belt moves towards the middle.

End: Now that you've figured out how to collect a MaxKare treadmill, you can partake in all the medical advantages of this machine. It's one of the most amazing collapsing electric treadmills for weight reduction, perseverance, and working on cardiovascular wellbeing. All the more strikingly, it has a most extreme weight breaking point of 220 lbs treadmill, making it an incredible choice for home use, particularly in the event that you've restricted space.

Habitually Sought clarification on some pressing questions.
1.Question How to turn on the MaxKare treadmill?
Plug the power line into a wall power source and search for the power switch on its casing. Press the power button into the reset position and stand on the machine's foot rails. Then, slide the clasp connected to the security key onto your garments' belt, embed the key into the treadmill control center and trust that the showcase will illuminate.

2.Question What is the most straightforward treadmill to collect?
Clients consider Skyline Wellness T101 Go Series the simplest treadmill to gather. Moreover, this wellness includes a calm engine and is profoundly strong.

3. Question How to lean the MaxKare treadmill?
MaxKare auto slant collapsing treadmill permits you to change its

slope level from 0 - 12%. Be that as it may, this is done physically, so you should get off the gear on the off chance that you wish to change the slope level. That's what to achieve, press the grade+ (increment) button once and press either the least speedy slope or grade - (decline) button to set the machine to the most reduced setting. Trust that the casing will quit moving before you get onto the treadmill.

4.Question What amount of time does it require to collect a MaxKare treadmill?

In the event that you have the right devices, gathering a MaxKare treadmill can take around 45 - an hour. Even better, you can advantageously collect the machine alone, yet it's in every case great to have a companion to take care of you.

CHAPTER 14..............INSTRUCTIONS To Pick Either Collapsing AND NON-Collapsing TREADMILL

Treadmills are the absolute most well known exercise machines available. However, more significantly, there are 2 kinds of treadmills relying upon their underlying models; collapsing and non-collapsing treadmills. Albeit the two choices offer incredible exercise meetings, while you're wanting to get one for your home, you should choose a specific sort. Anyway, what's the right treadmill to purchase? A great many people pick a collapsing treadmill for the undeniable explanation of saving space because of its minimal and fordable plan. Be that as it may, there are different viewpoints to consider while contrasting a collapsing Versus non-collapsing treadmill. That is precisely exact thing I'll check in this article out. Even better, I'll show you the advantages and disadvantages of every treadmill type to assist you with pursuing an educated choice.

Advantages of Collapsing Treadmill Models. Save space: The most remarkable thing about collapsing treadmills like An cheer 2 out of 1 collapsing treadmill is that they occupy less room contrasted with a non-collapsing machine. For that, they're an incredible choice for little spaces and home rec centers with restricted space. Additionally, you just have to overlap them up and store them away when you're not working out on the machine. **The most awesome aspect?** These exercise hardware have extra highlights like security secures that keep them when collapsed. Likewise, a couple of fordable treadmills either have a lifting framework or a computerized deck dropping framework to make them simple to crease.

Profoundly versatile: Collapsing treadmills are for the most part simpler to move around contrasted with their non-collapsing partners. Therefore, you can undoubtedly move them starting with one room then onto the next or take them with you while voyaging. What's more, as I referenced prior, a portion of these machines are even furnished with wheels, making them a lot simpler to ship. They make it simple to clean the house in the wake of working out One more advantage of fordable treadmills is that they make cleaning simpler. Basically crease up the machine subsequent to working out, store it away and clean or vacuum the floor region under the treadmill.

Reasonable: Fordable treadmills are an incredible choice in the event that you are on a tight spending plan since they're normally more reasonable than non-collapsing models. These treadmills, by and large, have a value scope of about $500 to $1000.

What Is a Non-collapsing Treadmill.

Not at all like fordable treadmill models, fixed or non-collapsing treadmills can't be collapsed and have a bigger impression. Albeit

this plan makes them less convenient, they're more steady, more grounded, and harder than their collapsing partners. All the more critically, their plan just elements fundamental parts like roller, belts, engine, and steel outline. Likewise, they cost more than fordable units as a result of their engine power, dependability, and in general nature of the machine. Simultaneously, these treadmills perform at the best quality, permitting them to oblige clients of different loads. Subsequently, non-collapsing units are usually utilized in sports centers and business treadmills.
Advantages of Non-collapsing Treadmill Models. Bigger engine and treadmill belt size Engine size assumes an essential part in deciding how strong a treadmill is. Fortunately, non-collapsing models ordinarily have a bigger engine than collapsing units. This permits them to oblige more client weight and offers a smoother, more predictable activity. Essentially, because of their enormous impression, non-collapsing treadmills have a more extensive belt. This gives clients more space and space to run or stroll on the machine.
Soundness: Soundness is a vital perspective to consider while searching for a decent treadmill. This keeps the treadmill from shivering or wobbling when you increment your speed. In addition, soundness guarantees that the machine feels strong and secure while strolling or running on it. All things considered, non-collapsing treadmills are more steady than collapsing units. This is on the grounds that they're furnished with highlights you may not find on a fordable treadmill for home utilize like substantial steel outline development, tough base, and so on. Furthermore, non-collapsing units are sturdier, more grounded, and have an incredible by and

large feel. Subsequently, treadmill clients can practice on the machine without it wobbling no matter what their weight.

Tips on Picking either Collapsing and Non-collapsing Treadmills.

With regards to accommodation, Collapsing treadmill models may be the preferred choice over non-collapsing models. Notwithstanding, non-collapsing units likewise offer a few particular advantages you can't disregard. To assist you with settling on the best choice, here are a few elements you ought to consider while looking at collapsing Versus non-collapsing treadmill models.

Cost: In the event that you're intending to utilize your treadmill routinely and for a sensible measure of time, you might need to spend more on the machine. For example, for running exercises, your base cutoff ought to be around $1,500. Be that as it may, in the event that you expect to involve the machine for strolling exercises, you ought to spend something like $1,000 on the machine. Security of collapsing treadmills versus non-collapsing treadmill models By and large, less expensive treadmills have a wobbly casing development. In any case, as you attempt to pick between collapsing versus non-collapsing treadmill units, you shouldn't set a financial plan that will drive you to think twice about. Likewise, take sure you leap, walk and run on the machine to check whether it gives a steady exercise routine. On the off chance that you feel the treadmill is adequately strong, its quality is great and ideal for your necessities. Fordable treadmill models ordinarily have decreased dependability contrasted with their non-fordable units because of their folding edge plan. Besides, they are furnished with a more modest base, making them less steady than collapsing treadmills. Accordingly, they normally wobble while working out, particularly assuming that you are running at high velocities. Thus, in the event that you need an exceptionally steady treadmill for rock solid exercises, non-collapsing treadmills are a superior choice.

Max Weight limit: Non-endlessly collapsing treadmill weight limit goes from 250 lbs to around 400 lbs. In any case, as far as possible recorded by most treadmill producers is presumably beyond what the machine can deal with. Consequently, you ought to deduct around 50 lbs from the prescribed weight ability to get a more sensible cutoff. Likewise, you ought to pick a machine with a higher weight cutoff to expand the treadmill's life span and try not to strain its engine.

Trans portability and capacity: Collapsing treadmills furnished with wheels on the base are not difficult to move around after work out. Plus, the greater part of these treadmills have a smaller plan, making them profoundly compact and fordable. Running against the norm, non-collapsing treadmills will generally occupy a great deal of room. This makes it important to have a non collapsing treadmill cover while you're intending to store them away. All things considered, to decide if to pick a collapsing or non-collapsing treadmill, you want to really take a look at the accessible space in your home. Likewise, consider the roof level since you'll be raising many creeps on the machine, particularly on the off chance that you're wanting to store the treadmill in a room with a slanting or low roof.

Collapsing or Non-collapsing Treadmill - Which is Best for You.
The conversation about which gym equipment is better, non-collapsing or collapsing treadmill, has been happening for quite a

while. Some treadmill clients guarantee that collapsing models are better since they occupy less room in the home rec centers and workplaces. While others accept non-collapsing treadmills are better since they will endure longer and are sturdier. All in all, which one do you pick? First off, one of the normal distinctions between collapsing versus non-collapsing treadmill units is that collapsing unit are more minimal. For that, they're not difficult to store away when not being used, making them the better choice assuming you are worried about space. For example, they're reasonable for individuals living in little spaces like lofts. Then again, collapsing treadmills are far in front of their non-collapsing partners in the event that you're worried about dependability. In particular, non-collapsing units have a bigger base, permitting clients to run at high velocities without making the machine wobble. **End:** To summarize, space, spending plan, and your wellness objectives are probably the main variables you want to consider while picking between a Collapsing versus non-collapsing treadmill. On the off chance that you have restricted space in your home, a collapsing treadmill with a more modest deck and tight space will be an extraordinary choice. Notwithstanding, you should likewise consider other key elements like deck padding, engine limit, weight limit, preparing projects, and decline/slant setting. No matter what the sort of treadmill you pick, both wellness machines will offer different advantages to your work-out daily practice. In addition, it's great to initially realize the distinctions among collapsing and non-collapsing treadmill models. This will assist you with finding the right wellness hardware that will suit your requirements and weight reduction or wellness objectives.

Habitually Sought clarification on some pressing questions.
QUESTION 1. What is the best collapsing treadmill from purchase's point of view? There are some great fordable treadmills available. They include: Go plus 2 out of 1 Collapsing Treadmill, Pro Form Brilliant Star 2000, TERRA Wellness TR-3500 Collapsing Treadmill.

QUESTION 2. How to crease a treadmill?
A few treadmills are outfitted with a fordable deck for helpful capacity and transportation. To overlap such treadmills, immovably hold the back finish of your machine. Then, at that point, cautiously lift the finish of its deck into an upstanding situation until its well being lock hook draws in to get the deck into position.

QUESTION 3. Might you at any point run on a collapsing treadmill?
Most fordable treadmills miss the mark on quality development and solidness expected to run at high velocities or longer distances. Notwithstanding, a few collapsing models have great parts that permit clients to run on the machine.

QUESTION 4. Do collapsing treadmills have a grade?
Numerous fordable treadmills give a grade scope of up to 12%, while others even give declines of up to 5%. In any case, a few fordable treadmills don't give slant settings by any stretch of the imagination. Thus, prior to choosing a particular collapsing treadmill, check whether it has slant/decline settings.

QUESTION 5. Are collapsing treadmills any benefit? Collapsing treadmills are viewed as an extra room saver, because of their fordable and minimal plan. Likewise, these machines are profoundly reasonable, making them an incredible choice for individuals on a careful spending plan. The best part is that a few fordable treadmills have great well being highlights and high level elements like calorie counting, pulse screen, and so forth.

CHAPTER 15…………….INSTRUCTIONS to Let Know If TREADMILL Engine IS Terrible

The treadmill engine is a fundamental part in the machine since it's liable for moving the running belt. Sadly, it's additionally one of the most costly issues to fix in your machine. Besides, a defective engine will make your treadmill quit working immediately and diminish the machine's productivity, keeping you from having a viable exercise. To keep away from such issues, it's fundamental to figure out how to let know if a treadmill engine is terrible. This will assist you with forestalling future free time by permitting you to make a move right on time before the engine is possibly harmed. All things considered, keep perusing this exhaustive manual for figure out how to check in the event that your treadmill engine is turning sour. You really want above all, this to realize about the treadmill engine.

The Treadmill Engine: The treadmill engine is liable for turning the running belt and is the absolute most significant part of an electric treadmill. That is the reason it's essential to think about the engine's sorts and quality while purchasing another treadmill.

Tragically, most treadmill engine specs just furnish you with their HP (Strength) rating. Be that as it may, there is quite a lot more data you ought to consider while purchasing a treadmill, particularly on the off chance that you need an exercise machine with a strong engine.

A portion of these perspectives are. Sort of engine: Two sorts of engines are regularly utilized in treadmills; AC and DC engines. AC engines produce considerably more commotion than DC engines and require a devoted electrical cable. In any case, they're very more impressive than their DC partners. For that, DC engines are by and large utilized in home treadmills, while AC engines are normal in business treadmills. One more remarkable distinction between these engines is that DC (Direct Current) engines utilize a commutator and brushes. Therefore, they need more upkeep, diminished life expectancy, and restricted speed due to extra wear things. Running against the norm, AC (Exchanging Current) engines utilize new, more modern innovation rather than brushes. Nonetheless, they're more costly however dispense with the requirement for supplanting the engine brushes 2 - 3 times each year.

Constant obligation Versus top engines: The constant obligation rating of a treadmill engine shows how much supported power during use yet not the real most extreme HP conceivable. At the end of the day, the treadmill engine will work at a similar power, whether or not you're running at 9mph or strolling at 2mph. Top obligation rating, then again, shows the greatest drive the engine can create and requires more energy to perform at higher speed rates. On the disadvantage, top engines break down much speedier than persistent engines since they're planned to be utilized for a more limited time frame. Additionally, they will quite often overheat whenever utilized too regularly or for a really long time, something you'll not insight with constant obligation engines. With respect to RPM, search for a treadmill engine that has less RPMs. This will ensure a higher force, expanded life expectancy, ideal execution, and better energy effectiveness.

Beat with regulation (PWM) : Beat with Balance (PWM) is an innovation used to control most treadmill DC engines. To be exact,

PWM engine regulators utilize a progression of On and Off heartbeats to drive the engine. Basically, when you put your foot on the running belt, the course of the engine turning the belt will be immediately hindered at a specific speed. Consequently, the PWM regulator will give a wide heartbeat to make up for this change, expanding the treadmill engine voltage. One advantage of involving PWM regulators in DC engines is that they're not generally so exorbitant as AC engines. Notwithstanding, on the disadvantage, the engine will be more vulnerable to overheating and exposed to a lot heavier pressure when a heavier client strolls at a more slow speed. Furthermore, this expands the possibilities harming the engine and the regulator.

Area of the treadmill slant engine: Not at all like the treadmill engine, the slope engine pushes you up while preparing on a treadmill, permitting you to run or walk uphill. Yet, more critically, it guarantees that you have an agreeable and reliable involvement in negligible vibration while preparing on the treadmill, no matter what the slope level and speed. Most exceptional treadmill makers put the slope engine at the focal point of the machine. This is the best area for the engine as it keeps the machine from moving side to side while you're running on the treadmill. As such, situating the grade engine at the focuses gives a significantly more even and stable insight.

Treadmill engine overheating: Treadmill exercises are probably the best cardio practices as they keep you sound and assist you with consuming a great deal of calories. On the off chance that the running surface or deck becomes more sweltering than typical, the engine might have a few issues. An overheating engine can prompt different specialized issues or even shut down the machine totally. All the more prominently, it might make the treadmill delayed down when you step on it. In any case, defective isn't the main issue that can make the treadmill overheat. Different causes incorporate; dust and garbage development between the deck and the belt and ill-advised grease. Aside from making the treadmill over, these variables will make the mechanical parts work proficiently, in this way dialing back your machine.

Belt isn't continuing on the treadmill: At the point when you switch on the treadmill, however the running belt doesn't move, something might be off with the engine. As a rule, this happens because of belt contact, dead engine, or loss of force association with the engine. On the off chance that a belt jam causes the issue, the machine will vibrate, however the belt won't move. All things considered, actually look at the internal piece of the deck and clean it to dispose of development dust. Moreover, utilize an excellent belt lube to grease up the treadmill belt properly.

The treadmill smells like consuming: A consuming smell is perhaps of the most reliable and boundless sign that your treadmill engine is turning sour. This bizarre smell ordinarily happens because of shortcircuits in the treadmill engine, wiring, and other electrical parts. Be that as it may, it could likewise be brought about by the contact and intensity created between the treadmill deck and belt while utilizing the machine. Whichever the case, in the event that you recognize any odd smell while utilizing your treadmill, switch it off immediately, turn off its power rope, check its engine and make the essential treadmill fix. In the event that the issue isn't brought about by the issues I've referenced above, clean the deck to

eliminate any dampness, garbage, and residue. A short time later, plug the power line back in and reboot your machine.
The presentation isn't working : In the event that your treadmill show isn't working, the engine or a free fitting might be an issue. Fortunately, fixing this issue with the control center showcase is moderately basic. To begin, check your machine's power link length and the apparent wires. Also, check for creased lines or worn batteries and supplant them. Besides, on the off chance that a free fitting causes the issue, turn off the power link, associate it back in and press the beginning button. Be that as it may, in the event that the above arrangements don't fix the issue, check the treadmill engine to appropriately fix any issues. On the other hand, completely look at the flywheel's attractive pickup and supplant the magnet assuming it has tumbled off. Also, the treadmill show may not be working because of the improvement of static in the control center. Assuming that is the situation, you might have to reset the electrical switch and turn off the power link for 1 moment to fix the issue.
Engine failure: A wasteful or non-working engine obviously shows it's turning sour. This will cause things like keeping the belt from moving proficiently while preparing on the treadmill. When you notice that your treadmill engine isn't proceeding as it ought to, ensure you check it right away. On the drawback, fixing a wasteful engine is one of the most costly treadmill fixes you'll at any point run. The engine keeps on working inadequately when controlled at max throttle; you'll need to supplant it. Or probably you'll encounter more issues like bombed circuits which can prompt wellbeing issues. Besides, it's suggested that you employ an expert professional to assist you with supplanting or fixing the treadmill engine or circuit.

Boisterous engine: Assuming your treadmill engine is making an irritating commotion, it could show that its engine has amassed gunk. Sadly, this additionally keeps the engine from really disposing of the created heat, accordingly influencing its general presentation. In this way, assuming you notice any clamor from your treadmill, actually take a look at the engine to check whether it's turning sour.

Inconsistent speed and non-working controls. Each mechanized treadmill is furnished with a proper arrangement of controls that you can use to run the engine or change the grade. On the off chance that any of these controls have quit working or are not working accurately, the engine has an issue. Notwithstanding, this issue can likewise be brought about by different issues like an exhausted belt. Whichever the case, assess the treadmill to check in the event that your engine is turning sour or on the other hand assuming you want to supplant the running belt. Soil and residue development in the engine On the off chance that you don't perfect the engine compartment routinely, residue and soil will collect inside your treadmill. This can prompt different issues like making the engine's inward parts overheat and resemble consuming.

Absence of support: Absence of standard upkeep is another normal issue that causes the treadmill engine to turn sour. This incorporates greasing up the running deck and cleaning the engine compartment now and again to forestall residue and soil development.

Instructions to Check assuming Your Treadmill Engine is Turning sour.

Like some other treadmill part, you don't have to purchase another machine in light of the fact that the engine is broken. All things being equal, you just have to supplant the engine. A few makers considerably offer lifetime guarantees on their engines. Nonetheless, it's essential to lead a tests first to analyze the genuine issue that might be making your treadmill engine turn sour. A portion of these tests incorporate.

Test treadmill engine with a multimeter: First of all, a multimeter is a gadget that actions a few electrical properties like obstruction, voltage, and flow in a gadget or circuit. A multimeter involves a DC and AC voltmeter, ammeter, and ohmmeter. Therefore, it's likewise alluded to as a VOM (Volt-Ohm-Milliameter). It's likewise worth focusing on that a multimeter utilizes different sensors in view of the electrical property you wish to gauge. For example, to gauge current, the gadget utilizes a galvanometer that behaves like a very delicate voltmeter. Oppositely, it utilizes a Wheatstone extension to quantify obstruction by contrasting the resistor's obstruction with an interior voltage. Furthermore, the gadget estimates voltage by contrasting it with an inside reference voltage. Before we take a gander at how to test a treadmill engine with a multimeter, it's essential to take note of that there are 2 sorts of this gadget accessible. That is advanced and simple multimeters. A computerized multimeter shows the deliberate worth on a mathematical presentation by means of a graphical bar, while a simple gadget shows readings through a moving pointer. Simple multimeters are frequently utilized for profoundly delicate circuits, while computerized multimeters are favored while recording a slight DC voltage change because of their precision. One way or another, multimeters are great for tracking down shortcomings with electrical parts or circuits and showing the ideal precision. The best part is that it will assist you with figuring out what portion of your machine isn't working.

With regards to treadmill engines, multimeters are basically utilized for 2 reasons. Test the force of the engine: A treadmill supplies capacity to the engine, which changes over that electrical energy into mechanical energy. Thusly, on the off chance that there is an issue with the power supply, the electric engine won't work as expected. Fortunately, as I've previously referenced, you can utilize a multimeter to supply test the engine's power. One thing you really want to note, however, is that this cycle and ideal evaluations can change contingent upon the sort of your treadmill engine. This is on the grounds that each engine has a normal voltage range, making it essential to test the wires to check assuming they meet those reaches. The treadmill engine voltage ought to by and large be somewhere in the range of 3.2V and 6.5V when the machine is running. **Review the engine windings:** In the event that you think your treadmill engine is having issues because of terrible shaft engine windings, a multimeter will assist you with testing that. In particular, the multimeter will assist you with testing the windings for wear and tear and break down their opposition. Besides, it's a speedy and simple method for testing on the off chance that your treadmill engine requires a full rewind or further testing. Nonetheless, before you utilize the multimeter to assess the engine windings, you want to set it to understand Ohms. A while later, test the engine's terminal and wires to review open/shorts in the circuit's windings and 'short to the ground.

Instructions to test the engine for 'short to the ground. To begin with, disengage the treadmill engine from its power source and set your multimeter to ohms. Then, utilize a screwdriver to eliminate the screws of the engine cover and get it off the machine. Whenever you've done that, cautiously detach the 2 wires prompting the power supply, remembering that the red one is generally DC lead. Then, test each wire and check for limitless readings. In any case, on the off chance that you get a perusing of 0, the issue might accompany the link. All things considered, you ought to test each link exclusively to figure out which link is terrible, it are not contacting to guarantee that their leads. Running against the norm, on the off chance that you get a limitless perusing with each link, you have an engine issue.

The most effective method to test for shorts/open in engine windings.
Test the T1-T2, T2-T3, and afterward T1-T3. Nonetheless, some treadmill engines have various markings like U, V, and W. assuming that is the situation with your treadmill model, begin with U-V, V-W, and finally, W-U. In a perfect world, you need a perusing of around 0.3 - 2 ohms. However, on the off chance that you get a zero (0) perusing, there is a lack in stages, meaning the links are short to ground. Then again, a perusing that is well over 2 shows that you most likely have an open winding or a wrecked wire. **Test the treadmill engine control board:** The treadmill engine

control board alludes to a little circuit board tracked down inside the treadmill. It comprises of different parts, including a chip, decoder, and memory for speed capacity. All the more critically, it guarantees that the machine generally chugs along as expected by guaranteeing the running belt generally turns at a reliable speed. To be exact, the engine control board screens the speed of the running belt and sends that data to the treadmill console, which then drives the engine. So for that, it's vital for keep the engine control board with everything looking great to guarantee that your treadmill works appropriately. Something invigorating about this part is that it doesn't need to be supplanted frequently. Regardless, typically a position can be handily gotten to and is accessible in many treadmills.

Surprisingly better, figuring out how to test a treadmill engine control board is somewhat simple since you can do it on the spot. For example, assuming the engine is murmuring yet the running belt isn't moving, the issue is with the engine control board. On the other hand, you can lift one finish of the engine get together, put it on a vibrating surface, and move the belt. On the off chance that the belt moves, the treadmill engine is practical. Nonetheless, the running belt won't move assuming your treadmill engine is terrible. **Actually take a look at the shaft and course:** Like some other electric engine, course are one of the most widely recognized parts to turn sour since they experience customary wear and tear. For that, it's vital to investigate them routinely and supplant them after some time. Besides, utilizing a treadmill engine with broken down orientation will diminish its proficiency and harm its functioning component. The uplifting news, however, is that course are not difficult to assess. In particular, you just have to pivot the course and check whether they're turning openly and easily. Likewise, you can move around the shaft the heading connect to. Assuming you feel any grinding, it's no time like the present you supplant the direction. In any case, on the off chance that the grating is minor, applying an ointment could assist with fixing the issue. **Assess the treadmill engine's fan:** The fan assumes a crucial part in the engine's presentation since it keeps it cool, permitting it to run for additional lengthy periods. Tragically, in the event that the fan is stopped up with garbage and residue, how much wind current moving to the engine will be diminished, hence keeping the delivered heat in. Thus, the treadmill engine will overheat and at last turn sour. That's what to forestall, it's great to consistently review and clean the fan to eliminate flotsam and jetsam and residue development. Additionally, keep the fan secure to the engine and test it to guarantee it pivots openly.

End: As may be obvious, a portion of the deterrent estimates I've referenced above are generally simple. To begin with, be that as it may, it means a lot to know how to check in the event that your treadmill engine is turning sour. All the more remarkably, a portion of these engine testing methods might need proficient support. All things considered, searching for a dependable expert you can contact when you think your treadmill engine is terrible is significant.

Habitually Sought clarification on some pressing questions. 1.Question For what reason is my treadmill belt not moving when I step on it? Different variables can make your treadmill belt quit moving when you step on it. In any case, this normally demonstrates that the distance between the 2 belt rollers requires change. Fortunately, you can fix this issue by changing the roller bolts with a hex spanner to move, relax or fix the back roller.

2.Question What amount does a treadmill engine fix cost?
The expense of treadmill engine fix will in general shift since fix experts as a rule have various costs. As a general rule, the treadmill engine fix cost can be somewhere in the range of $100 and $200. Then again, the expense of purchasing another treadmill engine goes from $200 to $300, selective of the maintenance charge. Thus, hope to spend more than $500 on another treadmill engine and substitution costs.

3.Question How long will my treadmill engine last?
As per most treadmill producers, electric engines utilized in these wellness machines can go on around 10 years. Be that as it may, you can make your treadmill engine last longer by greasing up the belt consistently and taking appropriate consideration of the machine.

4.Question What sort of engine do treadmills utilize?
Most home treadmills are furnished with a 80 to 260V DC engine with a reasonable drive rating and a PWM engine regulator. This permits treadmill clients to change the running belt speed and keep a consistent speed and great force while utilizing the machine.

CHAPTER 16…………….INSTRUCTIONS To Supplant Treadmill Belt

Treadmills are the absolute best wellness machines you can have in your home. They assist you with consuming calories, get more fit and remain in shape all through the year without agonizing over the brutal outside components. In addition, they're less arduous on the joints, permitting you to run with less gamble of injury. Notwithstanding, albeit most treadmills are intended to keep going for a really long time, a large portion of their moving parts can deal with 5 - 10 years of proceeded with use. The treadmill belt is the most weak part to wear and harm, making it break down and break after some time. Fortunately, producers have made it incredibly simple to supplant the treadmill belt once it gets broken down. Some treadmill proprietors even decide to supplant the belt to move up to a superior quality one. Whichever the case, before you embrace this undertaking, you really want to know how to supplant a treadmill. However, just relax! When you're finished perusing this aide, you'll effectively supplant any treadmill belt right away! To start with, how can you say whether your treadmill belt should be supplanted? We should begin from that point.

Signs That Your Treadmill Running Belt Needs Substitution.
As currently referenced, keeping your treadmill strolling belt in great

shape is significant, particularly on the off chance that you utilize the machine routinely. Nonetheless, it's not generally clear that the strolling belt is exhausted and should be supplanted. Hence, there are sure factors you ought to pay special attention to decide if it's the ideal opportunity for treadmill belt substitution Some of them incorporate.

Lopsided wear: An exhausted strolling belt makes the treadmill run less without a hitch or even harm the engine over the long run. To decide whether the belt is exhausted, release the belt and check for regions with lopsided wear on the two sides. Likewise, in the event that you find outrageous perfection on the running surface, you'll positively require another belt. The new belt will be significantly more sturdy and can endure higher rates and loads.

Frayed edges: Besides, assuming the belt has any critical deformity like frayed edges, cuts, tangles, and breaks, you might have to supplant it. In the event that vital, eliminate the treadmill belt and cautiously analyze it for any obscured patches. Simultaneously, search for smooth patches brought about by grating.

Free crease: Free creases in treadmill belts can break apart, causing serious injury while preparing on the machine. To check Are:

1. Run your finger along the belt's underside crease.

2. Look whether the crease is breaking into pieces, wearing, or fraying.

3. Consider supplanting your treadmill belt right away assuming that you experience any of these signs.

Belt slippage: A slipping belt will haphazardly reel you forward, making you stagger as you run on the treadmill. This makes it troublesome and risky to utilize the machine. Besides, it can cause the treadmill speed to dial back when you step onto the deck. Assuming you notice any of these issues, switch off the treadmill and investigate the issue. In certain examples, fixing the belt on the off chance that it's lifting for in excess of a couple inches will assist with tackling this issue. Nonetheless, on the off chance that that doesn't fix the issue, search for different choices like treadmill belt fix or substitution.

Ill-advised oil: The treadmill belt ought to be enough greased up to guarantee smooth and even development over the rollers. Plus, this will lessen grating between the belt and the deck, subsequently expanding the belt's toughness. To check in the event that the belt has legitimate oil, lift it the hard way and assess for extreme drying or wear. On the other hand, you can eliminate the belt totally to accurately examine it. On the off chance that the belt isn't exhausted, you can grease up it to keep it utilitarian. Be that as it may, assuming it's exhausted or gives any indications I've referenced above, you'll need to supplant it.

Age of your treadmill belt: Treadmill belts aren't intended to endure forever as they wear out over the long haul, consequently the need to supplant them. As a rule, how frequently you want to supplant the belt will rely heavily on how frequently you utilize the machine. On the off chance that you run on your treadmill consistently, you ought to supplant the belt each 1 - 2 years. Yet, assuming you use it sometimes, you can supplant it following 3 - 5 years. Putting resources into another moving belt will give a smoother, more predictable surface and increment your machine's life span. Be that as it may, it's essential to check your machine's strolling belt at regular intervals, regardless of whether it has no observable issues. Like that, you can rapidly recognize expected issues and make vital fixes before the machine totally separates.

The most effective method to Change a Belt on a Treadmill. In the wake of examining your treadmill and verifying that the belt should be supplanted, assemble the apparatuses you'll require for the assignment. A portion of these things include:

1. Set of Allen torques.
2. Phillips screwdriver.
3. Pincers.
4. Marker/Felt tip.
5. Another treadmill belt.

Whenever you've assembled every one of the required devices, follow these moves toward supplant the treadmill belt.

a. Turn off the treadmill: Before you examine the strolling belt, eliminate all electrical associations from your treadmill, including the wellbeing key, then turn off it. This disposes of the gamble of shock assuming you inadvertently press the button while supplanting the belt.

b. Eliminate the engine hood: Eliminate the screws holding the engine hood set up with your Philips screwdriver and concentrate it from the treadmill casing to uncover its parts. Then, utilize a screwdriver to relax the strain roller fasteners tracked down on the rear of your treadmill. This will relax the belt to permit you to feel its inside surface and assess its appearance.

c. Mark the roller position: In the wake of eliminating the engine hood, mark out the places of the back and front roller bolts with a felt tip or indelible marker. Then, utilize an Allen wrench to slacken the roller bolts to change the back and front rollers.

d. Eliminate the back and front rollers: Release and take out the screws on the two sides to eliminate the roller. Keep in mind, these are the very screws that influence the belt strain. Rehash a similar interaction to eliminate the front roller. When you eliminate the screws, you can take out the back and front rollers.

e. Eliminate the old strolling belt: Utilize the change bolt at the back of your treadmill to release the strolling belt. To begin with, guarantee the belt is sufficiently free to accommodate your hand under to actually look at the belt pressure. Then, eliminate the front roller change bolt, trailed by the old treadmill belt. Be that as it may, this technique may not work for certain treadmills, particularly top of the line models fitted with ride covers with a slide-mount or an under-mount. In the event that the ride covers don't have staples or bolts, don't eliminate them effectively. Yet, on the off chance that they have fasteners and staples, utilize a flathead screwdriver for popping the plastic deck on the right-hand side. Furthermore, assuming that the covers are held set up by screws, unscrew and eliminate them.

f. Eliminate the deck bolts: Take out the 3 or 4 deck bolts connected to the underside of your treadmill. Whenever you've done that, eliminate the back roller screws, plastic end covers, and the roller at the rear of your treadmill.

g. Eliminate the engine belt: On the off chance that your treadmill has a handrail on the right-hand side connected to the base, eliminate it first. Then, ask your accomplice or companion to hold the front roller near the pulley and lift the deck as you slide the strolling belt off the hardware.

h. Supplanting a treadmill belt: Before you introduce another substitution belt, guarantee the deck board surface isn't exhausted, and the floor is level. Also, clean the rollers to eliminate any wax or flotsam and jetsam. Presently, cautiously slide on the upgraded one and guarantee it's in the focal point of the treadmill. Additionally, check under it to guarantee it's impeccably situated in the center.

I. Supplant the back roller: Supplant the end covers and back rollers. Subsequently, put the back change bolts and the engine cover once again into position and secure them. For treadmill models with ride covers, you need to supplant them. On the other hand, you can utilize the screws to get the plastic side deck on the off chance that they were at first affixed or stapled down.

j. Belt-fixing: Set up the ride cover back and refasten the front roller belt. Then, pivot the change bolt with the Allen Wrench to fix the strolling belt. Ensure you return the change screws to the position you had stamped before prior to eliminating the belt.

k. Change the belt: Lift the treadmill belt with your finger in the center to check assuming that it has a proper snugness. For instance, a belt with the right pressure ought to just lift around 2 - 3 crawls from the treadmill deck. Assuming the hole between the belt and the deck is less or more than this, change it appropriately. Moreover, change the place of the treadmill belt. For example, in the event that it's excessively near the left, turn the left side at the treadmill's back to the right (Clockwise). Furthermore, assuming it's excessively near the right, turn the bolt to the left (counterclockwise) utilizing the Allen wrench until it's focused.

l. Test the treadmill: Subsequent to supplanting the treadmill belt, plug it back on and stroll on the machine at an exceptionally sluggish setting to look at on the off chance that it's working appropriately.

On the off chance that important, make the required changes and supplant the engine hood. For example, on the off chance that the belt slips when you stroll on it, turn the right and left changes once. Then, test the treadmill once more until you're happy with its presentation, then, at that point, set up its engine hood back.

m. Grease: Utilize a non-fraying, clean fabric between the treadmill deck and belt. That's what to achieve, push the fabric between the finish of the treadmill and the belt until you clutch the two sides of the strolling belt. Presently, drag the fabric to and fro over the length of the running belt 1 - twice. Apply a silicone oil added to the moving repertoire opposite to the engine cover around 6" from one side of the machine. Rehash on the opposite side of the belt. Plug in the treadmill, turn it on and stroll at a moderate speed for 5 minutes until the grease fans out equitably added to the repertoire.

The amount Does it Cost to Supplant a Treadmill Belt.
The expense of supplanting your treadmill, by and large, belt will rely upon the model and brand of your wellness hardware. Likewise, the expense might fluctuate relying upon whether you recruit an expert or introduce the best yourself. Nonetheless, it's crucial for check in the event that your machine is still under guarantee before you purchase another belt. A few makers offer service contracts on a few treadmill parts, including the belt. In the event that you're actually wanting to purchase a substitution belt, you ought to take note of that there are different choices accessible regarding cost and quality. By and large, the expense of getting another treadmill belt goes from $ 50 - $200. A similar case applies to the substitution and fix expenses. For instance, assuming that you enlist somebody to introduce the new belt for you, the substitution cost might increment

by about $100 - $150. Thus, the all out cost of treadmill belt substitution can be somewhere in the range of $150 and $400.
End: In general, supplanting a treadmill belt is a moderately straightforward cycle that you can do yourself. Notwithstanding, in the event that you've never gotten it done, it's great to look for help from somebody more knowledgeable about the assignment. All the more critically, look at the signs I've referenced prior to supplanting the belt. This will assist you with deciding if the belt should be supplanted or the issue can be fixed by a basic treadmill strolling belt fix. Whichever the case, it's critical to routinely investigate your treadmill belt to guarantee you have a protected and solid exercise.

Habitually Sought clarification on some pressing questions.
1. Question For what reason would it be a good idea for you to change the treadmill strolling belt?
Practicing on the treadmill strongly influences different machine parts, including engine and deck belts. Accordingly, the belt loses its lower or upper surface harshness over the long run, which can lead to certain issues. For example, broken down treadmill belts can break any time, prompting minor mishaps or falling. Simultaneously, it applies more strain on the engine and other treadmill parts, expanding its energy utilization.

2. Question What causes a treadmill belt to unexpectedly quit working?
Different variables can abruptly cause your treadmill running belt to quit working, beginning with mileage. Also, inappropriate treadmill belt establishment can make the belt fall off while utilizing the

machine. Ultimately, a failing engine can break the strolling belt, thwarting the machine from working appropriately.

3. Question How frequently would it be a good idea for me to supplant my treadmill belt? Treadmill belts begin to give indications of wear and tear over the long haul. Subsequently, supplanting them occasionally is significant, contingent upon how frequently you utilize the machine. By and large, a quality running belt can deal with 300 to 500 hours of purpose, which is around 5 - 10 years for most treadmill clients.

4. Question What sort of strolling belt would it be a good idea for you to purchase for your treadmill? To start with, decide the size of the belt you want by estimating its length and width. The width of the belt can be in millimeters or inches, however the length is normally in inches. All the more critically, the size of your substitution belt ought to constantly be equivalent to your old one to guarantee it fits appropriately. To get precise aspects, utilize a measuring tape to gauge the belt from its middle. On the other hand, check assuming the ongoing belt has aspects of its width and length on its underside.

5. Question Are all treadmill belts a similar size? As I've referenced above, you ought to guarantee that the supplanting belt is viable with your treadmill model. Sadly, treadmill belts aren't widespread and are accessible in different sizes. For the most part, you can track down belts 40 - 60" long and 13 - 22" wide.

Printed in Great Britain
by Amazon